JULIAN
OF NORWICH

Austin Cooper O.M.I.

JULIAN OF NORWICH
Reflections on Selected Texts

TWENTY-THIRD PUBLICATIONS
Mystic, Connecticut

North American Edition 1988 by
Twenty-Third Publications
185 Willow Street
P.O. Box 180
Mystic, CT 06355
(203) 536-2611

Originally published in Australia, copyright 1986,
by St. Paul Publications, Homebush, New South Wales.
Published in Great Britain in 1987 by Burns & Oats, Tunbridge Wells,
Kent.

ISBN 0-89622-366-3
Library of Congress Catalog Number 88-72017

Cover illustration: Stained glass window of Julian's cell at the Julian
Shrine in Norwich, England.

ACKNOWLEDGMENTS

Extracts from *Revelations of Divine Love*, translated by Clifton Wolters; *The Cloud of Unknowing, Prayers and Meditations of St. Anselm,* and *Meditations* by Marcus Aurelius. Reproduced by permission of Penguin Books Ltd.

From *The Four Loves* by C.S. Lewis, and *Self Abandonment to Divine Providence* by J-P De Caussade. Reproduced by permission of Fount Paperbacks.

From *Four Quarters* by T.S. Eliot. Reproduced by permission of Faber and Faber.

From *Pastoral Sermons* by Ronald Knox, and *Holy Wisdom* by Austin Baker. Reproduced by permission of Burns & Oats Ltd.

From *Confessions of St. Augustine*. Reproduced by permission of Sheed and Ward Ltd.

From *Teach Us to Pray* (published 1974) by Andre Louf, and *Jung and the Christian Way* (published 1983) by C. Bryant. Reproduced by permission of Darton, Longman, Todd Ltd.

From *Letter to an American Lady* by C.S. Lewis, and *The Greatest Drama Ever Staged* by Dorothy L. Sayers. Published by Hodder & Stoughton Ltd. Reproduced by permission.

CONTENTS

JULIAN
OF NORWICH

Introduction

"Who was Julian of Norwich?" people so often ask. And the answer must appear somewhat vague. There is much about her that we do *not* know: the exact dates of her birth and death, even her name (she is known simply from the Church of St. Julian in Norwich where she lived as a solitary); her family and social background. Despite this paucity of biographical data there are some things we can glean about her.

From her writings it can be deduced that she must have been born about 1342 and from other contemporary sources it is clear that she was still alive in 1413 and living in Norwich as an "anchoress." An anchoress was one who had chosen the life of a solitary, and lived a life of prayer. We know that in Julian's case she had the assistance of a maid (who is mentioned along with Julian in some contemporary wills) and that she counselled people who came to seek her advice. Indeed, Julian evidently exercised a significant ministry in this respect and we have the record left by one such client, Margery Kempe. But what we can still know about Julian is more valuable than a host of biographical facts.

When we read her *Book of Shewings (or Revelations)* we are introduced to a very intelligent woman who was well acquainted with Scripture and thoroughly instructed in doctrine. More than that, we can immediately know her as a person of great warmth and charm whose religious experience is expressed with vivid precision and gentle humanity.

In a host of colorful images she has much to tell us about her understanding of the human condition and our growth into godliness. She tells us, too, much about God, and her message can be only described as one of immense hope. Indeed, it is little wonder that the dour age of the Reformation almost totally ignored her. In subsequent centuries she was known to only a few, for she does not easily fit the mold of the age of Reason or the Enlightenment when God was often portrayed as a remote and almost detached observer. It has been left to our own age, with its deep (if hardly articulated) need for a god "so near...as the Lord God is to us" (Deuteronomy 4:7) to rediscover her.

In May 1373, Julian had a remarkable prayer experience which she recounted in her book, the *Shewings (or Revelations)*; after many years of further reflection on this experience she wrote a longer version of her work. The extracts in this book are all taken from this "long text."

In this little book the writer seeks to lead the reader through some of the teachings of Julian of Norwich by suggesting reflections on various short extracts from her writing. This is not offered as a theological commentary on Julian's teaching or a literary analysis of her prose. Indeed, the author wishes to express his debt to those who have labored to produce learned commentaries, in particular Edmund College O.S.A. and James Walsh, S.J.[1] Their two-volume work contains exhaustive notes and commentaries in addition to a critical edition of both the short and long text. Anyone interested in Julian's teaching must also be indebted to the commentary by Paul Molinari, S.J.[2]

The selections in this book have all been taken from the Penguin edition translated into modern English by Clifton Wolters.[3] This was first published in 1966 and thousands of people have become familiar with Julian's teachings through this modestly priced and very pleasing rendition. This text has been chosen for that reason, though it has been checked against the more recent version of Colledge and Walsh[4] and slightly amended, for example, in the precise dating of Julian's Revelation. In only a few cases have the words of the original been used.

There are indeed several contemporary editions and these bear testimony to the popular appeal of Julian in our time. There are evident similarities between her age and ours. The fourteenth century was in many ways a bleak period of disruption and breakdown: The ravages caused by the Black Death (bubonic plague) from 1348 are the most obvious. The swift and ugly death of as many as 40 percent of the population in some places and even more than 60 percent in others brought in its train not only profound social and economic consequences but also a great deal of fear, and not a few manifestations of religious excesses.

It was an ugly age in many of its aspects and the sense of dislocation was heightened by the confusion of the church. From 1378 to 1415 the Western church was divided against itself around two (and for a time three) competing popes. Added to all that, the Hundred Years War between England and France from 1337 was a running sore, and on the English scene the anti-papal statutes of 1351 and 1353 were symptomatic of the tensions in medieval Christendom, even before the schism, and point to the stirrings of national consciousness. And John Wycliffe and his views added further division and confusion to the church in England. Part of Julian's greatness is that she never gave way to gloom or despair, despite these contemporary trends.

Yet the age also had its great achievements. It is, after all, the period associated with the emergence of the vernacular. This was the age of Chaucer and Langland, and Julian certainly has her place among these great names of literature as well as one of those many great spiritual writers who adorn the fourteenth century. Julian well deserves study for her literary skill as well as her spiritual wisdom, and she merits the title "first English woman of letters." Her prose style and skillful imagery represent a great achievement in themselves. The Norwich that Julian knew was a thriving economic center, second only to London. The cathedral with its Benedictine priory and large library and the many houses of Friars made it a great center of learning too. It had a long tradition as a markedly Anglo-Saxon place, yet its close commercial ties with the continent ensured its being open to wider cultural influences.

How this historical context might have influenced Julian is a moot point. One thing is very sure: She comes across these centuries as a great Christian woman who has much to teach us and whose message reminds us of the beauty and joy that are inseparable from the Christian faith. It is hoped that these selections and short meditations will prompt the reader to turn to Julian's text: No selection can do justice to its variety and wisdom.

Sincere thanks to Mrs. Cheryl Grosser for her kind help and patience in typing the text; to the community at St. Mary's for much understanding and help; and to my mother for assistance with proofreading, and to whom this little book is dedicated.

Austin Cooper, O.M.I.

As this is intended as a devotional work, rather than an academic commentary, it seems preferable not to burden the text with numerous footnotes or references apart from these essential works:

[1] Colledge E. and Walsh J., *A Book of Showings to the Anchoress Julian of Norwich*, vols. I and II, Toronto, Pontifical Institute of Medieval Studies, 1978.

[2] Molinari, P., Julian of Norwich. *The Teaching of a 14th Century English Mystic*, London, The Catholic Book Club, 1958.

[3] Wolters C., (ed.) *The Revelations of Divine Love*, Penguin, 1966.

[4] Colledge E. and Walsh J., *Julian of Norwich Showings*, New York, Paulist Press, 1978.

CHAPTER 1

God Revealing

The first revelation tells of Christ's precious crowning with thorns. It included and demonstrated the Trinity, the incarnation, and the unity between God and the soul of man. There were many splendid revelations of eternal wisdom, and many lovely lessons about love, and all the subsequent revelations are based on these. . . .

The ninth relates the pleasure that the Blessed Trinity has in the grievous passion of Christ, and his pitiful death. In this joy and pleasure God wants us to be comforted and cheered along with him until we come to our fulfilment in heaven. . . .

The sixteenth affirms that the Blessed Trinity, our Creator in Christ Jesus our Saviour, lives eternally in our soul. There he rules in honour and governs all things; by his might and wisdom he saves and keeps us for love's sake; we will not be overcome by our enemy.

This revelation was made to a simple, unlettered creature on May 8, 1373...Chapters 1, 2).

All of us are the recipients of many blessings. Sometimes

these blessings are not immediately evident. We need to pause and discern them. It is especially in our prayer that we come to realize the truth of St. Paul's challenge: What have you that you did not receive? (1 Corinthians 4:7). Our very awareness of God is something that is given. It is God who first loves us (1 John 4:19) rather than we who make a discovery of God; it is God who first shows and reveals self to us in a multiplicity of ways, not we who "prove" God's existence as though we were working out a problem or completing an experiment. We do, of course, make our discoveries and are in fact "feeling our way toward him" (Acts 17:17), but we only "succeed in finding him" because God first knows, seeks, guides, and loves us.

Julian is very confident that she received such a "revelation" and that this revelation had Jesus Christ as its most significant element. He was the doorway, as it were, through which she caught some glimpse or some awareness of the mystery of God as Trinity. Julian is also very clear about the time of this revelation. It occurred on May 8, 1373, and she spent a good deal of her life pondering it and trying to elucidate its meaning for her; and from this experience she drew strength for herself and love for others. The God who was revealed to her was not an intellectual or philosophical abstraction but a vibrant and loving presence; like St. Paul, and indeed like all the great mystics, she was utterly confident of this God who revealed self to her: "I have not lost confidence because I know who it is that I have put my trust in" (2 Timothy 1:12).

While Julian is clear about the time and reality of this revelation, she is not equally clear about the means God used. Her own language suggests quite clearly that it was "seen," though in a variety of ways. Sometimes it was a question of bodily sight, at other times imaginative understanding or words found in her intellect and again at others by spiritual vision (see Chapters 9 and 73). Commentators have discussed these things at great length. For our purposes it hardly matters. We can be sure that God was revealed to Julian in several ways.

There are numerous ways in which God can "show" something and "reveal" self. Medievalists were used to brightly decorated churches and Franciscan popular piety had greatly encouraged visual representations of great truths, especially those concerning the life of our Lord. Julian could well have been given some special awareness of the mystical significance of something represented in such popular art. Her mind could have been suddenly enlightened concerning a special significance of commonplace things about her. Anyone well versed in the gospels would be familiar with such an approach; our Lord used a host of commonplace things in his parables to reveal hidden truths. Or again Julian's heart could have been especially enlivened by the power of some passage in Scripture. And there can certainly be those special prayer experiences of the mystics that cannot be adequately clothed in words. St. Paul, for one, was baffled by such an experience but sure of its reality (2 Corinthians 12:2). What really matters is that God is revealing himself in a variety of ways and that such experiences are not merely a matter of visual images, clear thoughts, or mere words:"The Good news...came to you not only as words, but as power and as the Holy Spirit and as utter conviction" (1 Thessalonians 1:4).

Julian's writing echoes such quiet strength and confidence. Although she does not clearly and consistently analyze the means God used, she is very sure of the special significance of that date, May 8, 1373. This specific and special event formed the basis of much of her reflection and prayer for the subsequent twenty years. It was a seed that only slowly grew to maturity.

It is useful for all of us to ponder the ways in which God reveals self to us: in the Scriptures, the sermons we hear, the living experiences we have, the beautiful things that come our way, the people we meet; the sudden illumination of mind and movement of heart that enliven us to the things of God. It is not always easy to catalogue the means of God's revelation. Very often we do not recognize the gentle presence of God entering our experience, indeed knocking upon it all the time. We are rather like the two disciples on the way to Emmaus. The identity of the stranger and the meaning of the message are only realized afterward. But as we remain faithful to prayer time, we are enabled to catch some glimpse of God's light shining through to us. Indeed, we can be very sure that the whole world is a sacrament of God's presence. John Henry Newman expressed this in his *Apologia:* "the exterior world, physical and historical, [is] the manifestation to our senses of realities greater than itself." And his great friend, John Keble, in the poem for Septuagesima in the *Christian Year* spoke of:

> The works of God above, below,
> Within us and around,
> Are pages in that book, to show
> How God Himself is found.

Doubtless in the lives of all of us there are moments and events of special significance. Sometimes we can instinctively appreciate this. It might be a time of great joy such as engagement, marriage, religious profession, ordination, a new job, or a friendship newly forged. Or it might well be an occasion of grief and sorrow, such as the loss of a loved one, a serious error of judgment and decision on our part, or loss of health or employment. There are many other occasions when we hardly see the significance that lies beneath the surface. But in the case of both types of events— the obviously significant and the apparently commonplace—it takes *time* to see something of their significance and to integrate such a revelation into our lives. For it really is a revelation; God is speaking to us in these events and supporting and nurturing us all the while.

So Julian shows us the wisdom of spending time in reflection and praying over events in our journey through life.

CHAPTER 2

Wanting God

Some time earlier she had asked three gifts from God: (i) to understand his passion; (ii) to suffer physically while still a young woman of thirty; and (iii) to have as God's gift three wounds.

With regard to the first I thought I had already had some experience of the passion of Christ, but by his grace I wanted still more. I wanted to be actually there with Mary Magdalene and the others who had loved him, and with my own eyes to see and know more of the physical suffering of our Saviour, and the compassion of our Lady. . . .I had no desire for any other vision of God until after such time as I had died. The reason for this prayer was that I might more truly understand the passion of Christ.

The second came to me with greater urgency. I quite sincerely wanted to be ill to the point of dying...I wanted to undergo all those spiritual and physical sufferings I should have were I really dying...my intention was that I should be wholly cleansed thereby through the mercy of God. . . .

There was a condition with these two desires: "Lord, you know what I am wanting. If it is your will that I have it. . . ."

As for the third, through the grace of God and the teaching of Holy Church I developed a strong desire to receive three wounds, namely, the wound of true contrition, the wound of genuine compassion, and the wound of sincere longing for God. There was no proviso attached to any part of this third prayer.

I forgot all about the first two desires, but the third was with me continually (Chapter 2).

While God reaches out to us, we for our part, respond in faith and hope and love. Our response is the other side of the coin of revelation. Revelation is a matter both of God's doing and our responding. And the response we make is a thing of gradual growth and increasing simplicity. Julian had some specific requests to make of God, yet gradually her response to God became more simple and single-minded. This is always the experience of the great men and women of prayer, and in recent times we associate it particularly with the Little Flower and her simple approach to the spiritual life. In Julian's time the anonymous author of the *Cloud of Unknowing* expressed it in a terse and practical way when writing about our loving response being simply "wanting God, and not what you get out of [God]."

Of course, even before that special experience of May 8, 1373, God was disclosing self to Julian, as indeed God does to all of us. As the psalmist tells us, God is "searching" for us:

O Lord, you search me and you know me,
you know my resting and my rising,
you discern my purpose from afar.
You mark when I walk or lie down,
all my ways lie open to you. . . .
Behind and before you besiege me,
your hand ever laid upon me.
Too wonderful for me, this knowledge,
too high, beyond my reach (Psalm 138).

And the Lord's knowledge of us and searching after us has only one purpose in view and is prompted by only one concern, and has about it an eternal abiding love: "He chose us in Christ before the foundation of the world that we should be holy and blameless before him. He destined us in love..."(Ephesians 1).

Each of us is already known to God, chosen before the foundation of the world and searched out by the loving God whom the poet Francis Thompson called the "Hound of Heaven."

Only gradually do we come to realize this abiding love of God.

Julian's first desire is comparatively simple. It began with Christ; and he must always be the beginning. It has a strong devotional ring to it. She wanted some understanding of the passion and to be "actually there" with the principal participants. Our initial response is generally devotional; that corresponds to the first human love, an affection for things tangible and close. We might well outgrow such devotions, but it can also be productive to return to them at times. They are part of the homely things of faith and enable us to be at ease with great truths and live comfortably on the frontiers of mystery. But Julian moves on to wanting more: With "some urgency" she wants to share Christ's sufferings. Faith might well seek dramatic expressions; it did with the young Teresa of Avila, and she outgrew it; it also did with Anthony of Egypt and remained his essential vocation. With Julian (as doubtless the case with most of us) something more mundane and ordinary was asked of her.

In her first desire Julian shows her growing love for the person of Christ, and in her second desire her growing generosity in giving herself to the Lord. But prayer gradually simplifies and Julian wants to be "wounded" in the sense of popular Franciscan piety, not by having a physical replica of the passion, but in the sense of a total personal change effected by the power of Christ's death and resurrection. Her third desire is, in effect, a prayer to know Jesus Christ and experience the power of his resurrection.

This third desire for the three wounds amounts to a whole summary of a life centered on prayer, a turning away from selfishness and sin through *contrition*, a heart attuned to the Lord in *compassion*, and an overriding and abiding search for God in all things and through all things. Her prayer life had simplified to simply wanting God and not wanting what she got from God.

Her journey through prayer will surely help all Christians to struggle with the multiple tensions, activities, and challenges of life; there does eventually emerge a simplicity of desire through the labyrinth of cares that can ensnare each one of us. Indeed, a consistent opening to God in prayer surely brings something of that peace that Christ has promised his followers. There is no gimmick to be employed here; nor is there any sure method of achieving this. It is a grace given. In prayer we wait on that grace of peace and simplicity; it will be given in God's time and in God's way. It is our task to wait patiently on the Lord. Simplicity of desire and unity of vision will eventually come to us.

The words of our Lord in the gospel are a clear reminder that the whole Christian approach to life can be very much simplified: "You shall love the Lord your God with all your heart, and with all your soul, and with all your strength, and with all your mind; and your neighbor as yourself. . . . Do this and you will live" (Luke 10).

Simply wanting God: loveable to self and in creation. We love god and others with the love God pours into our hearts. Most of us have a long way to go before we are so completely saturated in godliness. We know it is possible as we look at the experience of great men and women of constancy in prayer and wholeness in living.

When we come to our daily time of prayer, we so often seem confused, distracted, and restless. Indeed, that is what we often are. But as we persevere in giving this open space to God, our experience does alter. We can grow into a unity; our experiences can be centered and directed; out of the apparent chaos, the Spirit can bring peace and love.

CHAPTER 3

Waiting on God

And at once I saw the red blood trickling down from under the garland (crown), hot, fresh, and plentiful, just as it did at the time of his passion when the crown of thorns was pressed on to the blessed head of God-and-Man, who suffered for me. And I had a strong, deep conviction that it was he himself and none other that showed me this vision.

At the same moment the Trinity filled me full of heartfelt joy, and I knew that all eternity was like this for those who attain heaven. For the Trinity is God, and God the Trinity; the Trinity is our Maker and Keeper, our eternal Lover, joy and bliss—all through our Lord Jesus Christ. This was shown me in the first revelation, and, indeed, in them all; for where Jesus is spoken of, the blessed Trinity is always to be understood as I see it (Chapter 4).

The God Julian desires is also the God of whom she has had some experience. To some extent each one of us can identify with St. John's claim to have actually experienced "That which was from the beginning, which we have heard, which we have seen with our eyes, which we have looked upon and touched with our hands—concerning the word of life" (1 John 1).

In the many and varied ways of God, Christ had been given to Julian from her baptism and growth through a faithful life. In her extraordinary prayer experience on that May day Julian had her gaze turned toward this Christ who had been quietly revealing himself to her. In this prayer experience her vision became clearer. Now these earlier experiences seem to come to something of a climax in this "revelation." She naturally enough has this awareness of God as she looked upon Christ as he is the perfect image of the unseen God. And Christ images what God is like in his utter self-giving. He not merely reveals some information about himself, but he reveals himself by literally giving himself:

> His state was divine
> yet he did not cling
> to his equality with God
> but emptied himself
> to assume the condition of a slave,
> and became as men are;
> and being as all men are,
> he was humbler yet,
> even to accepting death,
> death on a cross (Philippians 2:6-8 JB).

Julian's prayerful awareness of this self-giving of Christ on the cross was so deep and penetrating as to be an immediate experience of God. As she says:

> *I conceived truly and mightily that it was*
> *him selfe that showed it me*
> *without any meane.*

Julian certainly saw something of that self-emptying in very graphic terms. But hers was not any morbid curiosity or overly sentimentalized piety: she has a very vivid grasp of Christ's suffering and something of the meaning of that suffering. Her knowledge, however, if not of a merely speculative kind, most certainly has an eminently practical quality about it.

Her gaze does not linger upon the suffering of Christ, but it shifts to the Trinity. When Jesus is seen, the Trinity is always implied: To be united to him necessarily involves a deeper and more mysterious relationship. In this prayer experience, Julian is aware of that joy, peace, gentleness, and love that floods the heart which is open to the Spirit (Galatians 5:22).

Julian quietly waits upon this mystery; she is humble and docile before it. And at this point our Lady, Mary, comes to mind:

> In my spirit I saw her as though she were physically present, a simple humble girl, still in her youth, and little more than a child. God showed me something of her spiritual wisdom and honesty, and I understood her profound reverence when she saw her God and Maker; how reverently she marvelled that he should be born of his own creature, and of one so simple. This wisdom and honesty, which recognized the greatness of her Creator and the smallness of her created self, moved her to say to Gabriel in her utter humility, "Behold the handmaid of the Lord!" By this I knew for certain that in worth and grace she is above all that God made, save the blessed humanity of Christ (Chapter 4).

Our Lady stands as the model of all who pray. She waited on the Lord and was prepared to be his handmaiden, his servant. Although young in years she had the profound wisdom to see something of herself—so fragile and small, and something of God her creator—so strong and enduring.

All who pray seek to wait patiently on the Lord. That is our first stance, and one that often seems to endure for a long time. One becomes, as it were, a fallow field awaiting the seed which is the word of God. Sometimes one waits upon God by quietly pondering the Scriptures; sometimes in reflecting on experiences—one's own or that of others who have explored the mystery of God; at other times the waiting can be by contemplating the beauty of a work of art, or marveling at the glory of God splashed across the physical world; sometimes, too, it is simply to face one's own darkness and uncertainty. We sometimes forget that Mary was "deeply troubled" by the word of God, as Luke tells us in his narrative of the annunciation. Waiting on God's word is not always a thing of superficial coziness; the peace it brings is a deep-down thing that takes time to grow. We all have to come to a realization of that basic fact, otherwise we throw off prayer as pointless and unproductive.

We have to face the fact that we can often seem to be confused and dithering as we ponder the word of God, and wait upon God. But we all need to remember two things about this business of waiting on God's word. The first thing is that God is doing something to us in this time; the seed of God has been planted in the field, but the field looks the same for quite some time. Nevertheless, the creative process is going on beneath the surface of things. And the second thing we have to remember is that the time we spend is love shown. However confused or dull it might seem, the time of waiting on God's word is never time wasted; the time spent is love shown.

God is doing something. The power of the Most High is overshadowing us; the Spirit is praying in us with words beyond our comprehension and power to utter (Romans 8:26). For our part, we assume the role of listener, one who waits, one who is open to receive. And in this oft-times tiresome process we learn patience and gentleness and self control; the Lord is healing and creating us as we wait upon him.

CHAPTER 4

Knowing God

It was at this time that our Lord showed me spiritually how intimately he loves us. I saw that he is everything that we know to be good and helpful. In his love he clothes us, enfolds and embraces us; that tender love completely surrounds us, never to leave us. As I saw it he is everything that is good.

And he showed me more, a little thing, the size of a hazelnut, on the palm of my hand, round like a ball. I looked at it thoughtfully and wondered, "What is this?" And the answer came, "It is all that is made." I marvelled that it continued to exist and did not suddenly disintegrate; it was so small. And again my mind supplied the answer, "It exists, both now and for ever, because God loves it." In short, everything owes its existence to the love of God.

In this "little thing" I saw three truths. The first is that God made it; the second is that God loves it; and the third is that God sustains it. But what he is who is in truth Maker, Keeper, and Lover I cannot tell, for until I am essentially united with him I can never have full rest or real happiness; in other words, until I am so joined to him that there is absolutely nothing between my God and me. We have got to realize the littleness of creation and to see it for the nothing that it is before we can love and possess God who is uncreated. This is the reason why we have no ease of heart or soul, for we are seeking our rest in trivial things which cannot satisfy, and not seeking to know God, almighty, all-wise, all-good. He is true rest. It is his will that we should know him, and his pleasure that we should rest in him. Nothing less will satisfy us. No soul can rest until it is detached from all creation. When it is deliberately so detached for love of him who is all, then only can it experience spiritual rest.

God showed me too the pleasure it gives him when a simple soul comes to him, openly, sincerely and genuinely. It seems to me as I ponder this revelation that when the Holy Spirit touches the soul it longs for God rather like this, "God, of your goodness give me yourself, for you are sufficient for me. I cannot properly ask anything less, to be worthy of you. If I were to ask less, I should always be in want. In you alone do I have all. . . ."

For just as the body is clothed in its garments, and the flesh in its skin, and the bones in their flesh, and the heart in its body, so too are we, soul and body, clothed from head to foot in the goodness of God. Yes, and even more closely than that, for all these things will decay and wear out, whereas the goodness of God is unchanging, and incomparably more suited to us. Our lover desires indeed that our soul should cleave to him with all its might, and ever hold on to his goodness. Beyond our power to imagine does this most please God, and speed the soul on its course (Chapters 5, 6).

The Judeo-Christian tradition has always asserted the goodness of creation. "God saw that it was good" is a biblical theme that runs from Genesis through the New Testament. The crown of this creation is the human person, made in the image and likeness of God. The goodness of God is proclaimed by the heavens, according to the psalmist, and in all this beauty and work of creation God "did not leave himself without witness, for he did good and gave you from heaven rains and fruitful seasons, satisfying your hearts with food and gladness" (Acts 14:17). The world is full of witnesses and hints about the goodness and loveableness of God and so St. Paul prompts us to take note of all these things: "Whatsoever things are true...honest...just...pure...lovely...of good report; if there be any virtue, and if there be any praise, think on these things" (Philippians 4:8).

There is a strong Christian tradition that emphasizes the goodness of the world of nature and people and sees it all as a revelation of God. St. Justin the Martyr says that "whatever is good belongs to us as Christians" and St. Gregory of Nyssa affirms that "God is everything that is good."

Julian, too, is very sure that God is everything that we know to be good; any goodness that comes within our experience is at once a pointer toward God and a sacrament of God. Thus, when she comes to give us her teaching on the Blessed Trinity a host of images crowds her mind and heart; so many revelations of goodness have come her way. In the first place is Christ, the perfect image of the unseen God, and he gives us the entry into the life of the Trinity: "We are able to pray to God because of his holy Incarnation" (Chapter 6).

But it is also true that much of Julian's experience of life speaks to her of the same reality. Her early upbringing, the acceptance, warmth, and affection she knew as a child now speak to her of the enfolding love of God; it is he who clothes, enfolds, and embraces us. The ease and affection with which Julian turns to these images of home and family more than hint at her own experience in her early years, and also show the ease with which she moves from them to a homely sense of God. She is utterly at home and at ease with the Triune God whose life we now share:

> We...are clothed from head to foot in the goodness of God (Chapter 6).

The wider world of created nature also speaks to Julian of this love of God. Her attention is also drawn to a tiny part of the created universe—a small hazelnut. She thought it so small and fragile that it would disintegrate were it not held securely in being. The hazelnut is an image, surely, of both the fragile individual and also the whole of the cosmos: "All is held in the firm embrace of God: The eternal God is your dwelling place, and underneath are the everlasting arms" (Deuteronomy 33:27).

We are being held and supported by the Maker, Keeper, and Lover. This is the firm ground on which we walk, the atmosphere we breathe. St. Paul did not hesitate to speak of the God in whom we "live, move and have our being" (Acts 17:28). By our baptism we are plunged into this life of God who is Maker, Keeper, and Lover. The Father is still Maker—the one who is creating and shaping us as the potter fashions an object: "O Lord, you are our Father; we are the clay, and you are our potter; we are all the work of your hand" (Isaiah 64:8).

He is also our Keeper, the one who is keeping us safe and secure because he is savior and healer, the one who reconciles us: "If anyone is in Christ, he is a new creation; the old has passed away...the new has come....God was in Christ reconciling the world to himself" (2 Corinthians 5:17-19).

He is our Lover. He is the one who accepts us, and whose love wraps us round like the air we breathe. "God's love has been poured into our hearts through the Holy Spirit" (Romans 5:5).

The Blessed Trinity is not merely the object of our contemplation, a great truth to be wondered at. It is more truly the very dynamism of our praying. We are accepted by God and the divine love is poured into our hearts by the Spirit who is the Lover. The Spirit quickens us, and brings us to life in Christ our Keeper, the one who saves. When we are reconciled through him we become adopted children, fellow citizens with the saints, no longer foreigners and strangers, but members of God's household, God's family. And so we are enabled to call God our Father in the most intimate and childlike manner. This Father to whom we go is the one who is the Maker, who sends us the creative Spirit.

To know the goodness of God, to experience God's self-giving and the sharing of life with us, is the "highest prayer of all" according to Julian. Her teaching prompts us to stop and allow the wonder of this truth about the Trinity to flood our minds and hearts. We are, here and now, through our baptism, caught up into the eternal rhythm of the life of Maker, Keeper, and Lover—Father, Son, and Holy Spirit.

Some part of our prayer should be a simple awareness of this life we now share and this dynamic pulse that gives the deepest and most enduring life to our being; it is a life we are called to experience and enjoy for all eternity.

Perhaps it is especially in the midst of challenges, temptations, frustrations, and storms that we especially need to stop and allow ourselves to be touched by this very comforting truth. The teaching of the psalmist would seem to bear this out:

> God is...our refuge and strength,
> a helper close at hand, in time of distress,
> ...though the earth should rock,
> ...though mountains fall into the depths of the
>   sea,
> ...though its waters rage and foam....
>
> The Lord of hosts is with us,
> the God of Jacob is our stronghold.
>
> The waters of a river give joy to God's city,
> the holy place where the most high dwells
> God is within it cannot be shaken (Psalms 46).

The storms of life can buffet the believer, and indeed must need do so. But such tempests are invitations to look within to those "Waters of a river" that give joy to the place where the Most High dwells. In some sense that must be the heart of the believer who is in this God, who is Maker, Keeper, and Lover. The truth is more fundamental and enduring than the passing storms. Such a prayer of a simple awareness of the Trinity within us and enveloping and embracing us is a fulfillment of the final command of this psalm: "Be still and know that I am God."

We all need to stop and wonder, to ponder the reality of Maker, Keeper, and Lover; to know Father, Son, and Holy Spirit. The revealed truth is not given us as some esoteric insight into the life of God; it is given us to be used.

CHAPTER 5

Filled with Grace

His will is that we go on knowing and loving until we are perfected in heaven....

So at the same time our Lord God, in order to teach this lesson, showed me Our Lady, St.Mary, and the true and outstanding wisdom which made her gaze on her Maker, so great, high, mighty, and good. The greatness and splendor of her vision filled her with holy dread, and caused her to see herself for the insignificant, lowly, simple creature she was compared with her Lord God. ...Because of this basic humility she was filled with grace and every virtue, thereby surpassing all creation.

All the time he was showing these things to my inward sight, I still seemed to see with my actual eyes the continual bleeding of his head.

...This revelation was real and lifelike, horrifying and dreadful, sweet and lovely. The greatest comfort I received from it was to know that our God and Lord, so holy and aweful, is so unpretentious and considerate. This filled me with comfort and assurance. ...As I see it the fullest joy we can have springs from the marvellous consideration and friendliness shown us by our Father and our Mak-

*er, through our Lord Jesus Christ, our Brother and
Saviour. ...no living man can know (this) unless it
is specially shown him by our Lord, or given him
by the inward abundant grace of the Holy Spirit.
Yet faith and trust and love earn their own reward... (Chapters 6, 7).*

And so Julian brings us back to our Lady, Mary. She is the
model of all who are serious about the Christian life of
prayer. Anyone who responds to God's call must be prepared to "go on knowing and living until we are perfected
in heaven." Our Lady is one who does just that. Hers was
the sort of response that was an ongoing one. This is the
glimpse we have of her in the Acts of the Apostles: "All
the apostles with one mind devoted themselves to prayer,
together with the women and Mary the mother of
Jesus..."(1:14).

The picture that emerges is of Mary, true to her vocation
to wait upon the coming of the Spirit, docile to its overshadowing when it comes to her, and faithful to keeping
the word which the Spirit implants in her. At its deepest
point this means that Mary was one who was faithful to
prayer. There was a deliberate consistency in her availability to the Spirit. She did not pray simply when she "had" to
or when she "felt" like doing so. With her this availability
to the Lord was an habitual attitude of mind and heart,
close to what St. Paul meant when he said we should "pray
without ceasing" (1 Thessalonians 5:17).

There is always a danger that we might imagine it is
enough to pray when we "feel like it" or judge ourselves
to be in the mood for it. Unless we develop some constancy and routine in prayer we cannot expect to grow into an
habitual attitude of mind such as our Lady had. If we only
pray when *we* feel or judge it to be worthwhile, then we do
not leave ourselves open to God in all our many moods

and frames of mind. Each day, each mood, each need must be left open to the Spirit; only some regularity in prayer will ensure that this is done.

For her part, Julian makes this sound something like a routine, and so it is. As she says, we are called to "go on knowing and loving until. . . ." This suggests some blend or harmony between praying and living, and between contemplation and action. And we must "go on" with the task of seeking this harmony. A great deal of the life of the committed Christian must be a persevering and loving devotion to the ordinary round of duties and common tasks. On the surface it appears as a dull routine, something perhaps of a "straightjacket." Yet it does bring its own strange freedom and joy; it liberates us from a trivial dependence on our own fluctuating feelings and changing moods. It does mean that we leave all these changing tides open to the gentle influence of God in a very personal and deliberate way.

Perhaps we Christians need to give much more thought to this call to persevere, and to stir up within ourselves the grace this call gives. The real test and witness of a specifically Christian love comes when we remain faithful to the task, no matter what tangents lure us aside. A real Christian love will mean that we battle through dryness, distraction, and dislocation and remain faithful to the tasks, the prayer, and the people who have a claim on us. It is at this level that our fidelity resembles God's fidelity; it is always there, whether it is appreciated, reciprocated, or rejected. A perseverance in prayer, to simply "go on knowing and loving until..." must surely lie at the heart of our quest for such a godly fidelity. The more faithfully we persevere in attentive prayer and loving work, the more we come to reflect the ever-present fidelity of God, whose love is always there. It is never subject to change or caprice.

As Julian presents it, Mary's fidelity seems to fuse together two great strands: the old Judeo-Christian tradition of "wisdom" and the contemplative tradition so rightly developed by the Eastern Fathers. Julian was made aware of the "outstanding wisdom" of Mary that made her "gaze on her maker." Fidelity to this contemplation does enable us to grow in wisdom. It gives us a measure of freedom from our limited and fluctuating selves and enables us to glimpse something of the creative work of God in our lives.

Mary certainly persevered in keeping God's word and in pondering it in her heart as a true contemplative. All the while she was growing. And her growth was at once a deepening self-knowledge and also a growing awareness of this creative, healing, and loving work of God in her life. The "holy dread" enabled her to see herself as so fragile, like the hazelnut; and at the same time she knew herself to be enfolded in the firm hand of the Maker, Keeper, and Lover. This is the basic realism, the most profound wisdom. It is knowing oneself in one's totality as a child of God. This realistic understanding of herself and of her God "filled her with grace and every virtue, thereby surpassing all creation." Mary is graced by the overshadowing of the creative Spirit, and is given the fullness of that Spirit whose fruit is known to us as

> Love...joy...peace...patience...
> kindness...goodness...faithfulness...
> gentleness...self-control (Ephesians 5:22-23).

As Julian sees something of the significance of the Blessed Virgin, she also sees as a backdrop, as it were, the "continual bleeding of (Christ's) head." This reassures Julian of the continual courtesy of God, and the fact that the risen Jesus, still bearing the marks of his passion is interceding for us before the heavenly Father. Because of this lasting work of Jesus Christ, we too have access to the Father and can grow in wisdom and grace as did our Lady. And so Julian affirms her belief that the fullness of joy can spring from this marvelous consideration and friendliness which is shown us through Jesus Christ, our brother and Savior.

The synthesis of all these apparently disparate elements

is a grace wrought by the inward working of the Holy Spirit. So much is given us. Yet Julian also sees that there is something that enables us to be rewarded: Faith, and trust, and love earn their own reward. This is one of those thoroughly refreshing statements which Julian can inject into her account of the spiritual life and which always breathes that essential quality of gentleness and homeliness so characteristic of her. Our faithfulness throughout life's journey, our continued trust in God even when things seem difficult and the monotony borders on boredom, and our loving prayer will all end in reward and thanks from God! For each of us will be addressed in those heartening (and surprising) words: "Well done, good and faithful servant."

CHAPTER 6

Grace Shared

More than anything else it is the loving contemplation of its Maker that causes the soul to realize its own insignificance, and fills it with holy dread and true humility, and with abundant love to our fellow Christians....

Throughout (this first revelation) I was greatly moved with love for my fellow Christians, that they might know and see what I was seeing, for I wanted to cheer them too. The vision was for all and sundry....

So I beg you all for God's sake, and advise you for your own, to stop thinking about the poor wretch who was shown these things, and with all your strength, wisdom, and humility look at God, that in his loving courtesy and eternal goodness he may be willing to show it to all and sundry, to our own great comfort. For it is God's will that you should receive it with great joy and pleasure, as if Jesus himself had shown it to you all (Chapters 6, 8).

As we have seen, Julian, like all the great spiritual teachers, insists that we must begin the Christian life with a real turning away from self. She had been willing to accept an illness involving great suffering: "I wanted to undergo all those spiritual and physical sufferings I should have were I really dying" (Chapter 2). At some stage or other we all have to accept some pain and suffering. For the most part we prefer not to seek it actively. Most of us have quite enough battling to do to accept it when it comes. But some real "dying to self" is essential for the Christian; and even the traditional human wisdom would agree that challenges, difficulties, and problems are necessary ingredients of character building. The Chinese have an ancient proverb that aptly sums it all up by saying "All sunshine makes a desert."

To "turn away from evil and do good" is a summary of the Christian way, or as St. John the Baptist put it in much more personal terms, "He must increase but I must decrease." There is always need for asceticism if we are to die to sin and selfishness and to be alive in Christ. One very real aspect of this asceticism is a commitment to a life of prayer. Prayer is not merely an aesthetic or therapeutic exercise for moments of intense feeling or times of worry and anxiety; it is a deeply creative activity that must involve the whole person, all his or her attitudes, feelings, and aspirations. A regular daily program of prayer ensures that the Lord touches all aspects of our life, and not merely those moments of intensely felt need or exuberant joy. This constancy in prayer involves a real discipline, but it is a discipline that eventually liberates and brings a deep freedom and prevents our being locked into our own passing emotions.

Julian makes it clear that "more than anything else" such a constant and loving waiting on the Lord brings about a true humility. This constancy in prayer teaches us much more about our own limitations and frustrations, our hopes and capabilities. This is the "true humility" Julian speaks of. We learn to know ourselves as we really are.

But the discipline of prayer involves more than a discipline and asceticism of giving time and place to the Lord on a regular pattern. It also involves us in a change of attitude toward other people. To pray is to be open to the outpouring of the Spirit of Love; it is to want to "put on Christ" and to approach others with his mind and heart; it is to open ourselves to the others with whom we call God "our" Father. At first sight all this involves a discipline. The fact that we pray commits us to treating others in a certain way. But it is more than just a discipline that we assume or a skill we train ourselves to perform. The way we treat others is a "natural" overflow of the love of God that has been poured into our hearts. So at first sight what seemed a discipline eventually becomes a real freedom. We gradually grow in love for our fellow humans, and that means a progressive liberation from our own self-centered world and from our own prejudices, fears, and tendency to manipulate and use others.

The real test of our life of prayer is the love we have toward other people as a result of our prayer. Julian calls it an "abundant love to our fellow Christians." Her deepening awareness of the Trinity moved her to love her fellow Christians and she wanted them to "know and see what I was seeing, for I wanted to cheer them too." The sort of love Julian experienced for others was not merely some dogged sense of doing good for others. It had about it a joy and spontaneity.

And as she experienced this great love for others, she also decreases in concern about herself. She does not want us to think about her; she is anxious that we turn our attention toward God, "that in his loving courtesy and eternal goodness he may be willing to show (this truth about the Trinity) to all and sundry for our own great comfort."

This concern for others is the sign of the genuineness of our prayer. The feelings we have are largely irrelevant, and not the final guide; the splendid thoughts and insights we might experience are only hints and suggestions about the mystery; the fervent desires we might articulate can all too easily wither before they flower into action. The real test of our prayer (and therefore of the quality of our Christian life) is the love we have for others. We have only to think of it in simple terms. If we immerse something in water it will get wet; if we saturate a piece of cloth in dye it will take on the color of the dye. It is the same with prayer. If it is *really* prayer, it is an immersion in the reality of God who is Father, Son, and Spirit. It is being clothed and embraced by Maker, Keeper, and Lover. Such an immersion must make us more godly, more like the God who is love. So our test of prayer is not so much its length, or its tangible fervor, or the profundity of its insights. We might simply *be* before the Lord, and feel very much like the "dry weary land without water."

But all the while God is doing something creative, healing and loving and molding us to be more godlike. We need to be very confident about the reality of our being-in-the-Trinity whenever we pray. This basic truth of the Trinity is the most important thing; the loving reality of God is doing something to us; the mystery in which we are involved is much more important than the few fragile and tangible hints we have of its presence. The few words we stutter or the fleeting thoughts we muster are not the whole story of our prayer. What God does for us is infinitely more significant than anything we do. In prayer we try to tune in to what God is doing.

Julian terminates this first revelation with some affirmations that show how confident she was about the "framework" in which our life and growth take place. There is a matter-of-fact acceptance of her own fragility; all the great teachers and mystics are sure that they are not good simply because they know something about the faith, or have "insights" beyond the ordinary. It is only love that makes the individual Christian good.

> *The fact that I have had this revelation does not mean that I am good....I am not trying to tell the*

wise something they know well already; but I am
seeking to tell the uninstructed, for their great
peace and comfort. And of comfort we all have
need. ...for I am united in love with all my fellow
Christians (Chapter 9).

This fundamental being-in-God reflects the teaching of St. John concerning the deep unity of all in Christ and with the Father (17:21-26) and this unity is made visible in the unity we have in the church. And so Julian makes an affirmation of belief in the church. That is part of this God-world in which we live.

For God is in man, and God is in everything. And
by the grace of God I hope that anyone who looks at
it in this way will be taught aright, and greatly
comforted if need be.

I am speaking only of those who are to be saved,
for in this matter God did not show me otherwise.
I shall always believe what is held, preached, and
taught by Holy Church. For the Faith of Holy
Church which I had understood from the first, and
which I hope by the grace of God I had consciously
kept and lived by, was ever before my eyes. I was
determined never to accept anything that was con-
trary to this, so it was with this well in mind that I
looked at the revelation so diligently (Chapter 9).

Julian evidently feels some uncertainty here: She must love "all" and those are the people to be saved. She does not look beyond that, nor has she any special understanding beyond that limit. She is quite ready to accept the limitations of understanding and accept the generally held teaching of the church. In a marvelously clear way she denies having any hidden secrets that might captivate the credulous, or excite those on the lookout for the bizarre in "private revelations." She frankly disclaims "any revelation or vision beyond the ordinary teaching of Holy Church."

In one great act of faith, Julian can accept the reality she is in: the God who is Maker, Keeper, and Lover and the ordinary world of church and people to be loved. This first revelation brings us to an understanding of Julian's basic realism, and prompts one to pray for a similar healthy attitude.

CHAPTER 7

Journeying Godward

(The Second Revelation)

After this I saw with my own eyes in the face of the crucifix hanging before me and at which I was ceaselessly gazing something of his passion. I saw insults and spittle and disfiguring and bruising, and lingering pain more than I know how to describe: and there were frequent changes of color. On one occasion I saw that half his face, from side to center, was covered with dry blood, and that afterwards the other half similarly was covered, the first half clearing as the second came.

All this I saw physically, yet obscurely and mysteriously. But I wanted to see it even more vividly and clearly. To my mind came the answer, "If God wills to show you more, he will be your light. You need none but him." It was he whom I saw and yet sought. For here we are so blind and foolish that we never seek God until he, of his goodness, shows himself to us. It is when we do see something of him by his grace that we are stirred by that same grace to seek him, and with earnest longing to see still more of his blessedness.

*So I saw him and sought him; I had him and want-
ed him. It seems to me that this is and should be an
experience common to us all.*

*On another occasion I was led in imagination
down on to the sea-bed, and there I saw green hills
and valleys looking as though they were moss-
covered, with seaweed and sand. This I understood
to mean that if a man or woman were under-sea
and saw God ever present with him (as indeed God
is) he would be safe in body and soul, and take no
hurt. Moreover he would know comfort and consolation beyond all power to tell (Chapter 10).*

In the first revelation, Julian placed us within the Christian context. Through Christ we know the blessed Trinity,
the God in whom we live, move, and exist. This also involves our having relationships and kinship with other
people, especially with all Christian people, that is the
whole church. This faith-world in which we live, however, can only be appreciated by some effort on our part, and
indeed by some consistent effort. There is a strong note of
urgency in Julian's oft-repeated insistence that we must
persevere in prayer, and her teaching on this has a strong
Benedictine flavor about it. A life of stability and a daily
commitment to a program of common prayer, *lectio,* and
work give the Benedictine tradition a strong note of regularity, routine, and consistency. Julian's own experience of
plumbing the depths of her revelations over many years
shows her practical commitment to such constancy in
prayer. Here too, in this revelation we come across hints
and clear affirmations of this.

In the first paragraph she tells us she was "ceaselessly
gazing" on the crucifix and in the concluding sections of
this chapter she tells us we must "seek with deliberation
and diligence" and "wait steadfast on him in love." Sometimes this might be a contemplative "gazing," sometimes

hard work demanding "diligence," but it will always mean being "steadfast." But it is important for us to realize that this life that involves some routine and consistency does not, thereby, involve stagnation; it is very much a life of growth and maturity, a development into our full stature as children of God.

The committed Christian is already *in* the mystery of God. How then can one describe the process of life and growth? Great explorers of the Christian way have used a variety of images. St. Gregory of Nyssa in his *Life of Moses* sees the mountain as a useful image of a life of prayer, a struggle upward to the mystery of God; Walter Hilton gives us the image of a ladder, while St. Teresa of Avila uses the notion of the many mansions. All of these and a host of others echo the Scriptures and give us hints about the mysterious encounters of these great men and women of Christian experience. Julian does not have any one, single image but invites us to explore more deeply the mystery we are already living and experiencing. In this sense, Julian's approach is much like that suggested by T.S. Eliot, in the final section of the *Four Quartets*, where he also (later) quotes her:

> We shall not cease from exploration
> And the end of all our exploring
> Will be to arrive where we started
> And know the place for the first time.

Julian is sure that her knowledge is only partial and cannot always be neatly packaged and labeled:

> *All this I saw physically, yet obscurely and mysteriously.*

She makes us very much aware that our life of faith is a strange mixture of something already possessed, seen, and experienced, and at the same time something still to come. It is a gift of the very real substance of the faith, a life in God; yet it is also something still to reach its completion, something to be hoped for. Or, as St. John has it, "We are God's children now; it does not yet appear what we shall be" (1 John 3:2).

The journey of exploration into God is one that will make us traverse familiar scenes again and again. It is rather more like going round in circles than traveling in a straight line. And that certainly makes it a challenge for Westerners whose minds are conditioned and whose expectations are shaped by more than a century of notions about "progress." C.S. Lewis, in a somewhat different context, has an image that seems to suit the Julian approach. In *The Four Loves* he writes:

> Let us suppose that we are doing a mountain walk to the village which is our home. At midday we come to the top of a cliff where we are, in space, very near it because it is just below us. We could drop a stone into it. But as we are no cragsmen we can't get down. We must go a long way round; five miles maybe. At many points during the *detour* we shall, statically, be far further from the village than we were when we sat above the cliff. But only statically. In terms of progress we shall be far "nearer" our baths and teas.

There are moments on our journey when things are evidently going well, when we see something for our striving, and have a sense of satisfaction. They are moments for which we can be genuinely grateful; it's good to get the occasional cheering glimpse and hints of things hoped for. But often, too, we will be passing through rather familiar territory, perhaps on the farther side of the mountain and don't seem to be getting very far, or indeed getting anywhere at all. That is just the way we see things. Often we seem to be on the far side of the mountain, well out of sight of home, perhaps struggling again with old problems that we thought well settled and removed from our path. Julian had some partial baffling glimpse of the suffering Christ;

the faith traveler has only partial glimpses, baffling hints. But on this darker side of the mountain, God is still the light for the pilgrim, the cloud by day and the fire by night.

So as we make this journey of faith we can be sure that we are safely in the hands of God. Julian makes use of the image of the depths of the sea, an infrequently used one in Scripture, but in Sirach 24:7 and Psalm 68:22 it is clear that God has control of things even in those most mysterious of regions. This whole process of Christian growth and redemption is a baffling one for Julian as her own words make clear:

> *This secounde shewyng was so lowe and so little and so symple that my spirytes were in great traveyle in the beholdying, mournyng, dredfull and longyng: for I was some tyme in a feer wheder it was a shewying or none.*

However, her persevering fidelity eventually facilitates the gift of peace. All that matters is "his will"; whether he is "seen" or "sought" hardly matters for the pilgrim:

> *For God's will is that by faith we should see him continually, though it seems to us that we are seeing him so little. By this faith he makes us ever to gain grace. His will is to be seen; his will is to be sought; his will is to be awaited and trusted (Chapter 10).*

Julian makes passing references to Veronica's veil. From it she knows the features of Christ were disfigured because of human sin; God's will for us is that in our new creation in Christ we, like him, will pass from being disfigured to being "like our Saviour Jesus Christ." It is a sign of Julian's wonderful spiritual maturity that the details one might cull from Veronica's veil are of no interest to her. Much more important is the fact that we are journeying from darkness and disfigurement to a complete re-creation in the risen Lord. This journeying will mean that sometimes we are given glimpses of God-light; at other times we are in darkness and lack of meaning. But something more emerges that enables Julian to hold these two in a joyful and serene tension:

Seeking is as good as seeing.

Throughout this journey we are really walking with God. All we can do is "seek, endure and trust." But this is done by the power of the Spirit: "And all this the soul achieves by the Holy Spirit." So whether we are on that part of the journey that involves seeking, or whether we are enabled to see something, it is all the same: "Seeking is as good as seeing." The peace Christ promised as his one tangible gift to his faithful followers becomes the underlying reality that enables the Christian to hold these seeming opposites in a productive harmony.

And so Julian gives us some very practical teachings about the business of seeking and seeing:

> *The work that this vision depicts is twofold: seeking and seeing. There is nothing very special about seeking. It is a thing that every soul can do with God's grace, and do with the common sense and teaching of Holy Church. God's will is that we should do three things in our seeking: (i) that by his grace we should seek with deliberation and diligence without slacking, and do it moreover gladly and cheerfully without moroseness or melancholy, (ii) that we wait steadfastly on him in love, and do not grumble or gird against him in this life—which is not very long anyway—and (iii) that we trust him wholeheartedly and confidently. This is his will (Chapter 10).*

So we are all pilgrims, journeying Godward along a path that sometimes is shrouded in mystery and darkness, and at other times bathed in light. What really matters is that we persevere in this pilgrimage, accepting both the seeking and the seeing. Julian is so right: As we seek diligently and wait steadfastly, we will grow in a wholehearted confident trust.

CHAPTER 8

No Doer But He

(The Third Revelation)

After this I saw the whole Godhead concentrated as it were in a single point, and thereby I learnt that he is in all things. I looked attentively, seeing and understanding with quiet fear. I was thinking "What is sin?"

For I saw that God in fact does everything, however little that thing may be. Indeed, nothing happens by luck or chance, but all is through the foresight and wisdom of God. If it is chance or luck to us, it is because we are blind and shortsighted. Things which God's wise foreknowledge saw before creation...break upon us suddenly and take us by surprise. And because of this blindness and lack of foresight we say they are chances and hazards. But they are not so to our Lord God.

Hence it follows that we must admit that everything that is done is well done, for it is Our Lord God who does it. How God functions in his creatures was showed me at this time; not how they function in themselves. God is the focal point of everything, and he does it all. And I was sure he does no sin! (Chapter 11).

Julian completed her account of the second revelation with the assertion that God will appear "unexpectedly" and that God "works in secret, yet wills to be seen." For our part we must "seek with deliberation and diligence" and "wait steadfastly" in great trust and confidence. The journey Godward has these two sides to it. God is working secretly and silently like the leaven in the gospel parable (Matthew 13:33). God will appear at a time we least expect it. The human side of this mysterious journey is that we wait in patience and seek with diligence. As we seek to hold this double truth in harmony, we need to remember that God is always the first to move; God first loves us; the initiative is always God's. There will come those precious moments when a ray of light bursts through the clouds and we see something of God's purpose and plan, and something of the divine creative and saving presence.

Such a moment seems to have come to Julian at this stage. This was a matter of "understanding" and not any sort of physical or imaginative vision. She had seen some very homely images of God working in her life, and some sign, too, of the suffering servant whose pain was both "horrifying and dreadful, sweet and lovely" (Chapter 7).

Her language is different now. She appreciates something of the utter simplicity of God, who cannot be adequately contained in, nor totally identified with, the familiar and homely images she had used. It is to be expected that Julian will have recourse to more abstract and philosophical terms in her effort to articulate what must always remain beyond the power of human language of whatever kind. In most of her images, Julian sees God as Beauty, Truth, or Goodness. Now God is seen as the One.

"The single point" is Julian's way of expressing this utter transcendence and perfect simplicity of God. It is just this that at once means that God is not absolutely identified with any one thing or many things, but is able to be in all things, supporting them by power, creating them by wisdom, redeeming them by love.

While Julian is deeply aware of sin, and is asking herself how can sin exist along with this omnipotent and omnipresent love, she is content to leave off any treatment of that for the present. The much more realistic thing is to be assured of the presence and the loving wisdom of God. In this, Julian shows us the very great wisdom of leaving the mystery of divine hands and not seeking instant answers or solutions.

Here, in one sweep of faith and vision, Julian sees that God is both utterly "other" than the world of things and events, yet also in some mysterious sense entwined in the web of events. She manages a wonderful balance between the ideas of God's transcendence and his immanence.

As Martin Buber says in *I and Thou:*

> Of course God is "wholly other" but he is also wholly Same, the wholly present. Of course he is the Mysterium Tremendum that appears and overthrows, but he is also the mystery of the self evident, nearer to me than my I...If you hallow this life you meet the living God.

Julian is very sure that the "wholly other" is also close, indeed within each of us. And Eckhart in the *Threefold Life of Man* asserts the same truth: "God is closer to me than I am to myself; and he is just as close to wood or stone, but they are not aware of it."

Our own myopic view can mean that we do not always see as much of the grandeur of God's plan and purpose in events as we might. We can be rather like someone with our nose so close to the page that we do not see the meaning of the words, let alone catch a fleeting glimpse of the hand of the author. How right Julian is to say that we are "blind and short-sighted."

Part of our prayer is to ponder the mystery of the events of our own life and times; so often it seems a hazardous jumble of cruel fate, good luck, and the mere monotony of routine and duty. But Scripture gives us another side of the coin to ponder. There is always a wisdom at work. "Though she is but one, she can do all things, and while remaining in herself she renews all things; in every generation she passes into holy souls and makes them friends of God, and prophets "(Wisdom 7:27).

There is some sense in which it can be said of everything that God did it; "there is no doer but he." Everything is either ordained directly by God in some way or permitted. Nothing happens that is outside the scope of God's permissive will. As we confront the mystery of evil and sin and innocent suffering, we are unable to come up with a satisfying intellectual answer; but in the contemplation of the passion of the Lord we know that God is identified with the human condition in a deeply personal way. In the end, our being able to live at peace with this mystery depends on our ability and readiness to live with The Mystery—the reality of God and the divine, living providence. This is the wisdom of the believer who affirms: "The works of the Lord are all good, and he will supply every need in its hour. And no one can say 'This is worse than that,' for all things will prove good in their season"(Sirach 39:33-34).

And with the psalmist we can say:"Great are the works of the Lord" (Psalm 111:2).

The final answer given by Julian to the world's apparent "chances and hazards" is to believe firmly in the eventual triumph of good, and *that* is assured by our faith in the God whose loving mercy enfolds and embraces us. For the man or woman of prayer, the final "solution" to the problem faced by these "chances and hazards" and the evil and destruction they often bring is to assert the underlying reality of the Blessed Trinity. Julian's final words in this vision (Chapter 11) is to echo again her clear teaching on the Maker, Keeper, and Lover in whom we live and move. God is not ceasing to uphold creation and be, in some deeply mystical sense, "in it."

> *Nothing shall fail of his purpose. He made all things in abundant goodness, and therefore the Trinity is for ever satisfied with what he has done.*

> *He showed me all this to my great happiness, as if he were saying, "Look, I am God. I am in all. I do everything! I never cease upholding my work, and I never will. . . ."*

CHAPTER 9

Through Combat

(The Fourth, Fifth, and Sixth Revelations)

God through his compassionate love has made an abundant supply of water on earth for our use and comfort, he wishes us to use quite simply his blessed blood to wash ourselves clean of sin. For there is no comparable fluid that he would so like to give us. Of all it is at once the most copious and most costly (because it is divine), and, because of his great love, it is the most suitable and gladdening we could want. . . .

It is his passion that overcomes the Fiend, and...the Fiend is as evilly disposed now as he was before the incarnation. However hard he works, just as often he sees all souls escape him, saved by the worth and virtue of Christ's precious passion. This is grief and shame to him, for whatever God allows him to do turns to our joy and to his shame and woe. . . .

His power is in God's control....

After this the Lord said, "Thank you for all your suffering, the suffering of your youth. . . ."

The Lord, I saw, occupied no one place in particu-

lar in this house, but presided regally over it all, suffusing it with joy and cheer. Utterly at home, and with perfect courtesy, himself was the eternal happiness and comfort of his beloved friends (Chapters 12, 13, 14).

But how does one really know this underlying reality of God quietly and firmly supporting us beneath the "chances and hazards" of life? How can our awareness be something more than a mere notional assent? In our journey Godward we *can* become more sure and confident of the ground on which we walk, the way we follow. All great men and women of prayer have become increasingly confident of the great fundamental truth, the primordial mystery, God. The only way for the believing Christian to grow in this confidence is to identify more and more with Christ who is the "way." He is the map we follow on our Godward journey, the compass that sets us unerringly toward our goal. He alone can lead us through the darkness to the light. And his way is a way through suffering to glory, through death to resurrection.

In the fourth revelation Julian turns her gaze toward the body of Christ, "bleeding copiously," apparently as a result of the flogging. This is different from all her other pictorial images of the suffering Christ. Elsewhere she concentrated on the crucifixion itself. And in looking at the bruised and battered body of Christ two images converge: an "abundant supply of water" and his "blessed blood to wash ourselves clean of sin." The image of water is a natural one for life, like the tree planted beside flowing waters in Psalm 1. In Scripture it symbolizes our salvation: the destruction of evil in the flood, the safe passage through the Red Sea. The waters of baptism are cleansing and they immerse us in the death and resurrection of Christ; and in the vision of St. John the mystic, we are washed clean in the blood of the lamb (Revelation 7:14).

To reflect on our baptism is to deepen our commitment to the fact that we are saturated in the Christ event. This is a truth about ourselves, a fact of our Christian existence. We *are* a new creation, born again of water and the Spirit. This truth is given us for our "use and comfort" and needs to be pondered and wondered at in our times of prayer. Baptism is not a remote event of our past; it is a present reality, a gift "most copious and most costly...the most suitable and gladdening we could want." Our baptism was a beginning, a seed we must nurture and nourish. Sometimes in our prayer we need to renew and deepen this reality of baptism.

> Do you not know that all of us who have been baptised into Christ Jesus were baptised into his death? We were buried therefore with him by baptism into death, so that as Christ was raised from the dead by the glory of the Father, we too might walk in newness of life (Romans 6:3-4).

Doubtless part of our prayer could well be a *lectio divina* use of the baptism liturgy. One can only have some longing for the great practical teaching available to Christians who used places of worship such as the baptistry of the Cathedral at Ravenna, Italy. In celebrating baptism there, one is surrounded by all the great images of initiation into Christ. Somehow we need to allow the power of the many images of baptism to take hold of our Christian mentality once again. The liturgy of baptism is a storehouse of images that reminds us of what we *are:* people who have renounced evil, have been plunged into the waters and risen again, clothed in the symbolic white robe, anointed with oil and given the lighted candle. These are not empty rituals but life-giving symbols we can re-tap. Baptism is a grace we possess, a life we live that can be rekindled, renewed, and deepened in prayer. It is a grace that needs to grow and develop to maturity. St. Cyril of Jerusalem reminds Christians "You have been admitted to the divine life-giving baptism and are now capable of receiving the more sacred mysteries."

With this fact of our being in Christ ever more firmly in our grasp, we can face the presence of evil in the world and in ourselves. Julian tells us at the beginning of the fifth revelation that, "God allowed me to look at himself for a considerable time" and then he framed in her soul the words "By this is the Fiend overcome." She had a growing confidence in our new life in Christ. That new life is a sharing in the death and resurrection of Christ and we Christians are immersed in that mystery through baptism. But evil exists. Julian quite clearly saw that the Fiend is "evilly disposed" and works hard. But the pain and confusion he can cause can be turned to joy. However powerful evil might be in our world and in our hearts, it is a power that is in God's control. But there is a spiritual combat; we must battle with the powers of darkness and destruction; they have a hold within us. But still we affirm the power of Christ's victory over evil and our ability to choose it or reject it:

> If we have died with him we shall also live with
>   him;
> if we endure we shall also reign with him;
> if we deny him, he will also deny us;
> if we are faithless, he remains faithful—
> for he cannot deny himself (2 Timothy 2:11-13).

In the third of these revelations Julian's tone changes dramatically. She looks beyond the temporary struggle and the pain that evil causes. She also sees the reality of victory.

The Lord thanks us for our suffering. Once again Julian adverts quite naturally to the homely courtesy of God. And so we take consolation in our struggle with evil, so often a half-hearted struggle, and one in which the waters seem to reach high and threaten to engulf us. Yet God's grace is sufficient for us, and his power is made perfect in our weakness (2 Corinthians 12:19). This somewhat muddled effort of ours will earn the reward and thanks of God. We will hear the cheering words, "Well done" (Matthew 25:21).

The images of the Lord "at home" is surely reminiscent of the Father in the parable of the prodigal son. In that loveable figure there was nothing other than the warmest of welcomes. He saw the son afar off, ran to meet him, kissed and embraced him and saw him as "found" and "alive." There were no bitter recriminations, no demands, no awkward questions, indeed no punishment imposed. The Father displays all that is meant by being at "home"; perhaps the best image that we have to describe heaven. There, the love that God has poured into our hearts, and which we must share with others, will be seen and experienced in all its beauty. Julian sees it in terms of the perfect homeliness and courtesy of God.

So in our pilgrimage Godward we need to return again and again to the great truths of our being: We are redeemed in Christ; we do struggle against the power of evil, which cannot vanquish God; we are destined for a heavenly homeland.

CHAPTER 10

Through Pain

(The Seventh Revelation)

After this he treated my soul to a supreme and spiritual pleasure. I was filled with an eternal assurance, which was powerfully maintained, without the least sort of grievous fear. This experience was so happy spiritually that I felt completely at peace and relaxed: nothing on earth could have disturbed me.

But this lasted only a short while and I began to react with a sense of loneliness and depression, and the futility of life; I was so tired of myself that I could scarcely bother to live. No comfort or relaxation now, just "faith, hope, and charity." And not much of these in feeling, but only in bare fact. Yet soon after this our blessed Lord gave once again that comfort and rest. ...then I felt the pain again; then the joy and pleasure; now it was one, and now the other many times—I imagine quite twenty. . . .

The will of God is that we should know he keeps us safely, alike "in weal or woe". . . .Both are equally his love (Chapter 15).

Julian is very much aware that there are moments when we have some felt appreciation for the things of faith. There are indeed moments when the beauty of Christian art, the grandeur of church architecture, the attractiveness of music and prose can lift our minds to the things of God. And we have all known times when either liturgical worship or our own private prayer was accompanied by feelings of peace and well-being. Julian obviously had some such feelings, and they were very intense indeed, so intense that she thought "nothing on earth could have disturbed me."

But it is not in the ways of God to leave the Christian in such uninterrupted composure. And how very vibrant and clear are her words describing the desolation that engulfed her: "loneliness, depression, futility of life. . . ." At one time or another we have all felt these pains, or something like them. What is the meaning of it all? How do we cope with it and make it productive? As we read on in this chapter it becomes clear that Julian has analyzed as best she could the causes for this aridity. She was clear that such feelings are not always the result of sin. However, it is possible that we may have acted in a destructive manner; we might well have brought these feelings upon ourselves by sin. But that is not always the case.

Perhaps we can best understand something of the meaning of the dryness and desolation if we imagined life without any such moments of pain. Would we be satisfied? Perhaps we might be lulled into a superficial round of activities that would buffer us from the harsher realities of life. It is hard to see how such an unruffled existence could lead us anywhere but to hardness and selfishness; we would have to preserve the peace, *our* peace, at whatever cost. As it is, we do spend a great amount of effort trying to do so. But God does not leave us wander in such a desert without the occasional call. God breaks through into our narrow self-complacency and breaks down the defenses we seek to erect to ensure a tranquil life.

There is always the danger, too, that we will be so taken up with the consolations and gifts that come from God that we would rest contented with them, rather than seeking the God from whom all these good things come. The feelings of loneliness, depression, and futility of which Julian speaks are nothing other than God being present in a special way. God is prompting us and leading us to see that something deeper is needed than these doubtless pleasant feelings we would like to cling to. We are being weaned off these and invited to search deeper. Julian now gives us another of her teachings in which she shows that the Christian can indeed go deeper, beyond surface impressions and superficial feelings and discover God in the depth of one's being. In Chapter 10, she has taught us that "Seeking is as good as seeing"; now we are taught that God keeps us safely

alike in "weal and woe"...both are equally his love.

There are times when our world seems to come unstuck, when the waves of "loneliness...depression...futility" and the rest sweep over us. In such times we need to keep our minds on the "bare fact," as Julian tells us, to remember the great truths we saw in the last chapter: We are in Christ; we must confront the evil in the world and in our hearts; we are being led toward our everlasting home. These are truths much more real and factual than any emotions and feelings we might have from time to time. The Lord will lead us to treasure these truths more deeply as he leads us through the darkness of this death-to-the-senses. It will not be learned all at once, this lesson. We will have to be brought back to it time and again. But each time we will go a little deeper into the Mystery of God. As we look back on these moments we learn that God's love is present *equally* in "weal or woe."

CHAPTER 11

Learning Compassion

(The Eighth Revelation)

It was after this that Christ showed me something of his passion near the time of his dying. I saw his dear face, dry, bloodless, and pallid with death. It became more pale, deathly and lifeless. . . .

For at the same time as our blessed Lord and Saviour was dying on the cross there was, in my picture of it, a strong dry, and piercingly cold wind. . . .

The pain, sharp and bitter, lasted a very long time, and I could see it painfully drying up the natural vitality of his flesh. . . .And it seemed to me, that with all this drawn-out pain, he had been a week in dying, dying and on the point of passing all that time he endured this final suffering. . . .

Because of all this I was able to understand something of the compassion of our Lady St. Mary. She and Christ were so one in their love that the greatness of her love caused the greatness of her suffering. In this I found an example of that instinctive love that creation has to him—and which develops by grace...most fully and supremely shown in his dear Mother. Just because she loved him more

than did anyone else, so much the more did her
sufferings transcend theirs. . . .All his disciples and
real lovers suffered more greatly here than at their
own dying. . . .

There were times when I wanted to look away
from the cross, but I dared not. For I knew that
while I gazed on the cross I was safe and sound...
(Chapters 16, 18, 19).

In Chapters 16-21 Julian gives very vivid descriptions of
the pain and suffering experienced by Christ in his last
hours on the cross. There can be no doubt that in many
ways this account displays a wonderful familiarity with the
details of Scripture. There was a "strong, dry and piercingly
cold wind," which accords well with St. John"s record of
the bitter cold of those last days of Christ's life on earth:
The servants and officers were "warming themselves"
(18:18). But it also symbolizes the fact that the cause of suffering and pain can often be external to ourselves. The
piercing wind suggests the manner in which sufferers are
the innocent victims of circumstances.

The descriptions of Christ's pain in dying are perhaps
more detailed and vivid than contemporary people might
like to dwell upon. Yet Julian lived in a time when there
was much suffering, and the horrors of the Black Death
(1348, 1351, 1360) still stalked Europe. In our day, too, we
are accustomed to graphic and detailed news accounts of
the ravages of famine, drought, and violence in so many
parts of the world. Like Julian, we can also be very sure
that God is at the center of the pain, suffering, and cruelty
of the contemporary world. The story of the crucified one
is not something we can politely blur with the mists of
time. There is still ugliness and squalor and abuse of people, and God is still in the midst of it in some mysterious,
loving, and saving way.

Part of Julian's description centers on the fact that Christ was being dehydrated. Here again the word from the cross "I thirst" (John 19:28) provides a firm scriptural basis for her meditation. Her description of this process:

> *And the payne dryede uppe all the lyuely spyrites of Cristes flessh.*

Colledge and Wash render this as "And this pain dried up all the vital fluids of Christ's flesh." This sapping of the vitality of Christ struck Julian as a lengthy and drawn-out process as though the few hours of the passion were in fact a full week.

The draining of Christ's vitality stands in contrast to the copious supply of water and the grace of baptism. It reminds us that we have been bought with a price:

> You are not your own;
> you were bought with a price (1 Corinthians 6:20).

> There is one mediator. . . .
> the man Jesus Christ;
> who gave himself a ransom for all (1 Timothy 5:6).

> ...you were ransomed...
> not with perishable things such as silver or
> gold, but with the previous blood of Christ (1 Peter 1:18).

So for Julian this painful death was a prolonged process. Doubtless, any time of suffering does hang heavy; it is slow and ponderous. And there in the midst of this sad-laden time is the figure of Mary. She took her stand beside the cross of Christ. When others fled or made excuses and denials, she deliberately took her stand beside the cross. In her compassion she, too, felt the weight of the pain-time. All followers of Christ are called at some stage to take their place and simply remain with the suffering. For Our Lady there was no questioning as she had done at the Annunciation. There is no asking "how," no anxious searching as when Christ was at length found in the temple, no embarrassed concern as at Cana. There are depths of grief that are beyond the power of words to explain or assuage. And everyone who would be alive in Christ has to experience this and simply stay with the pain. For all of us this pain-time seems so much longer than any other time, and the call is to stay with the pain. Sometimes it might be the sight of death and pain in loved ones, as it was in the case of Mary on Calvary. At other times it might be the pain of the circumstances: the chill winds of misunderstanding, hostility, or failure that sap our energy. Sometimes, too, it might be pain within us, internal tensions and failures that cry out for healing and hope. Worst of all, there might be times when the darkness seems to have totally obliterated our awareness of God. Dorothy L. Sayers touched on a style of "death of God" attitude when she wrote in *The Greatest Drama Ever Staged:*

> Perhaps the drama is played out now, and Jesus is safely dead and buried. Perhaps. It is ironical and entertaining to consider that once at least in the world's history those words might have been spoken with complete conviction, and that was on the eve of the Resurrection.

Meanwhile, the Christian remains quietly on his or her own Calvary, learning the compassion of Mary and also learning the secret, mysterious, and unspeakable power of hope.

It is only natural that there are times when we want to turn away from the suffering and seek some form of escapism, a spiritual tranquilizer or antibiotic that will deaden the pain or make us forgetful of it, if only for a time. We moderns are very keen on instant solutions. But in the deeper things of the spirit there is no instant solution to pain and suffering. Although she wanted to turn away from the cross and from suffering, Julian knew the Christian solution: to stay with the pain. While she gazed on the cross she knew she was "safe and sound."

To many this is sheer "folly"; but to those seeking the Christian way the cross is "the power of God" (Philippians 3:18) but actually to "glory" in it (Galatians 6:14).

CHAPTER 12

Hope of Glory

(The Ninth and Tenth Revelations)

...suddenly, while I gazed on the cross, his expression changed to cheerful joy! ...We through our own pains and passion, are now dying with him on his cross, and that as we deliberately abide on that same cross, helped by his grace, to the very end, suddenly his expression shall change, and we shall be with him in heaven.

...The sharper our suffering with him on his cross, the greater our glory with him in his kingdom. . . .

This experience lifted my mind to heaven, and I saw there to my amazement three heavens...all contained in the blessed humanity of Christ....

The first heaven that Christ showed was his Father, not in any physical representation but as he is in his nature and mode of working; that is to say I saw in Christ what the Father is like. . . .

And here, for the second part of my threefold vision of the passion, I saw that the love which made him suffer is as much greater than his pain as heaven is greater than earth. . . .

And here I saw the last part of my threefold vision of his passion, the joy and happiness that delighted him. ...It is the will of Jesus that we should think carefully of the happiness of the Blessed Trinity over our salvation, so that we too, by his grace, should desire to have equal happiness. ...As if he were saying, "It is sufficient joy and delight for me to know that I can truly satisfy you. I ask you nothing else as the result of my suffering."

In this way he caused me to think about the essence of giving cheerfully (Chapters 21, 22, 23).

While Julian gazed on the cross she saw a change in the countenance of Christ. For a long time it must have seemed to Julian that nothing in particular was happening. So our prayer and life must often be: a "gazing," a fixing of the mind and heart on the Lord and those we must serve. This is particularly so when there is evident pain and suffering involved. All the while we can be sure that a change is being effected.

The Scriptures show us that there is a real progression and development in the revelation of the meaning of suffering. This is particularly shown in our reading of the four gospels. In Matthew and Mark there is the traditional picture of Christ, the suffering one: Sorrow, desertion by friends, and betrayal are themes that dominate the narratives. At the Last Supper Jesus said "One of you will betray me." Here, in the midst of a meal, so deeply symbolic of friendship and trust, there is a powerful note of tragedy and sorrow. In the garden he revealed his deep sorrow and anxiety of mind: "My soul is very sorrowful, even to death." Then on finding his friends asleep yet again, he told them, "Behold, the hour is at hand, and the Son of man is betrayed into the hands of sinners." These two authors note the silence of Jesus in face of ridicule and also the way Barabbas is preferred to Christ. And then come the terrible final darkness and Christ's words, "My God, my God, why have you forsaken me?" This was all real suffering and no mere semblance.

In Luke an added aspect emerges. Here we see the great compassion and tenderness of Christ and his concern for others. He told his disciples he "longed" to eat this Passover with them; in the garden he healed the ear of the high priest's servant when it was cut off in defensive anger; when a "great crowd" followed him to Calvary he told them, "Weep not for me but for yourselves and for your children"; on the cross he spoke the words of mercy: "Father, forgive them, for they know now what they do"; and he promised the good thief the grace of paradise.

In John's Gospel there is a different emphasis again: God is clearly in this world of suffering, and God has it firmly in his keeping. John tells us that "Jesus knew that the Father had put everything into his hands, and that he had come from God, and was returning to God" (13:3).

Here, Jesus is King; and the sign Pilate had affixed to the cross is used as a clear testimony of fact. Here, in John's Gospel, we have another revelation of the glory of God, seen in the midst of the pain and suffering.

It is one historical event, but it has different layers of revelation. Julian seems to see something of this great variety of inter-related truths in the one event. There are times of pain and darkness, and the Christian has to heed the call to remain with this pain and darkness. As Julian has it, "Through our own pains and passions...we deliberately abide on that same cross." But we, too, shall see that the pain turns to joy, the darkness gives way to light, and the shame becomes the glory. Julian's suggestion that this will happen "suddenly," as it happened in her vision, suggests both the grace of transfiguration and also an allusion to St. Paul: "We shall all be changed, in a moment, the twinkling of an eye" (1 Corinthians 15:51). Meanwhile, we must be prepared to await with great hope the full revelation of God's kingdom. But there is, as Julian rightly asserts, a real connection between the extent of our suffering here and the glory we will experience there.

In the midst of the sufferings of the present time we keep our eyes firmly fixed on Christ; in him we already have the fullness of the Kingdom; in him we have been given all good things. So we can identify in faith with the joy of Paul in proclaiming: "Blessed be the God and Father of Our Lord Jesus Christ, who has blessed us in Christ with every spiritual blessing in the heavenly places" (Ephesians 1:3).

And to see Christ is to come to know the Father. "I saw in Christ what the Father is like." Through the life, death, and resurrection of Christ we know what the Father is like; we know he is present in the midst of human suffering and pain; we know he is reaching out in compassion and love; we know that he is bringing all things and all human experience to a fullness and completion; his glory is being revealed.

And, as Julian rightly sees, the whole Trinity is involved in the work of our salvation and is rejoicing over it. She adds the cryptic remark: "In this way he caused me to think about the essence of giving cheerfully." So we come back to the effect that prayer must have on the Christian: a greater love for one's fellows. The joy that the Trinity knows in our salvation should overflow in our actions toward others. This is a thing of heaven. There is joy in heaven when the sinner does penance (Luke 15:7). So our love and care for others is not a mere stoic duty or a routine task; it is to be done cheerfully. And that demands a lot from us.

In the tenth revelation Julian saw "his blessed heart riven in two" (Chapter 24). Again she stresses this as a joyful thing, a revelation of the love of God. She sees this as "his sweet enjoyment" and the expression of his "delight in your holiness and in the endless joy and happiness you share with me." This is so different in tone from much writing on the Sacred Heart in more recent centuries. It is also in marked contrast to much contemporary devotion that tended to stress the morbid and the ugly. Julian stands as a refreshing corrective to much popular devotion in the period after the Black Death.

Julian adds a very real qualification to our devotional life in this revelation. Devotions are always subjected to contemporary fads and attitudes. This is inevitably so, for devotions are the human emotional response to the things of faith. Only slowly are these purified and given more clarity as vehicles through which the light of Christ shines on the human condition. One has only to think of numerous medieval cults of places and holy people. These were popular responses and it took time for Christianity to "baptize" them, and more time for them to grow into Christian maturity. Julian is one of those very rare people whose "devotion," that is, whose affective and emotional response to the things of God is generally balanced, and has about it a timeless Catholic quality. Her stress on "joy" has a thoroughly New Testament ring to it.

CHAPTER 13

Foretaste of Glory

(The Eleventh and Twelfth Revelations)

...with this same cheerful joy...(he) brought to mind the place where our Lady was standing during his passion. "Do you want to see her?" he said... "for after myself, she is the greatest joy I can show you...."

Jesus, in that word gave me, a spiritual sight of her...he showed her, exalted, noble, glorious, and pleasing to him above all creation. . . .

After this our Lord showed himself, in glory even greater than I had seen before...(Chapters 25, 26).

In these two revelations Julian gives us some inkling of her appreciation of our call to glory. Our Lady is seen in the full flowering of the grace that had been given her. That was a grace made clear at the Annunciation; it was matured through the pain of exile in Egypt, and through the challenge of her son's mysterious identity and ministry, and brought to completion in her faithful stand during the dark hours on Calvary. Now she bears the marks of glory. She has fully grown into her calling as the highly favored one to whom God has done great things. In many ways it all sounds very far removed from our own experience and struggles.

T.E. Eliot once wrote that we humans cannot take "too much reality." We can only know the greatness and the beauty of God when it is refracted for us in hints and symbols. The collect for the feast of the Transfiguration in the Eastern church stresses the same fact:

> Christ our God
> you were transfigured upon the mountain
> and showed your disciples your glory
> as they were able to bear it:
> kindle your everlasting light upon us sinners
> by the intercession of the Mother of God.

She who has been able to stand the weight of glory because she heard the word of God and kept it is well suited to intercede for us that we might see the glory of God being revealed in the warp and woof of our own lives. St. Peter reminds us that he, James, and John were on the mountain of Transfiguration and had some glimpse of the glory:

> ...for we were with him on the holy mountain. And we have had the prophetic vision made more sure. You will do well to pay attention to this as to a lamp shining in a dark place, until the day dawns...(2 Peter 1:18-19).

The great men and women of prayer have climbed mountains most of us could never hope to scale and have discerned distant horizons most of us can hardly imagine. We do well to keep in mind the reality and validity of their vision of the things we are striving after. They have caught some glimpse and hint of what "no eye has seen nor ear heard" (1 Corinthians 2:9).

We need to remind ourselves that we too are being "transfigured from glory to glory" (2 Corinthians 3:18). We are involved in a process of growth that must make us more human and thereby more nearly an image and likeness of the Father. The glory of Christ in his transfiguration was that he was recognized, accepted, and loved as the Son of the Father: "This is my beloved Son...." That, too, will be our glory, to be recognized, fully accepted, and loved as children of the Father without spot or blemish. Our Lord's transfiguration is not a remote event or a contrived poetic image. It is the meaning of our human growth and our destiny—glory. C.S. Lewis in *The Weight of Glory* rightly chides us that our vision might not be sufficiently lofty:

> We are half-hearted creatures, fooling about with drink and sex and ambition when infinite joy is offered us, like an ignorant child who wants to go on making mud pies in a slum because he cannot imagine what is meant by the offer of a holiday at the sea. We are far too easily pleased.

We pray that Julian's vision of Our Lord's glory and the final transfiguration of Our Lady may enliven our vision and lift our sights beyond the petty and frustrating to the great design in which we are all involved. If, like St. Peter, we seek to keep this vision alive in our hearts, then the petty and frustrating things take on a new significance: They become the instruments whereby we are refashioned after the image of Christ. As de Caussade remarked: "God teaches the heart, not by ideas, but by pains and contradictions."

In these chapters Julian rightly challenges us to lift our sights beyond the annoying and challenging, and above the distracting and passing, to deepen our appreciation of our destiny. She has often repeated that God is everything that is good (Chapters 8 and 9) and that there is no rest in anything less than God; he is our true rest (Chapter 5). It is all very reminiscent of St. Augustine's affirmation at the beginning of the *Confessions*: "You have made us for yourself and our hearts find no peace until they rest in you."

To this point in her book, Julian has brought us to the

stage where we need to gather together all our experiences into the life we share in Christ and the goal of the journey we travel with him. In the face of this, all else should gradually fade into insignificance for the Christian. Here is the final simplicity we seek in our prayer. St. Paul puts it this way:

> I count everything as loss because of the surpassing worth of knowing Christ Jesus my Lord. For his sake I have suffered the loss of all things, and count them as refuse, in order that I may gain Christ...(Philippians 3:8).

The mystery of the transfiguration challenges us to hold in some tension the reality of the present moment and the reality of the call to glory. The former might often seem ugly, tiresome, a dull monotony, or at best trivial and commonplace. But it also contains the germ and seed of glory waiting to burst forth. This is the cause of our joy. In this revelation Colledge and Walsh translate the description of Our Lord as the appearance of "mirth and joy" (Chapter 25). We need to pray for the grace to catch some glimpse of the mystery of transfiguration.

CHAPTER 14

Sin

(The Thirteenth Revelation)

In my foolish way I had often wondered why the foreseeing wisdom of God could not have prevented the beginning of sin, for then, thought I, all would have been well....But Jesus, who in this vision informed me of all I needed, answered, "Sin was necessary—but all is going to be all right; it is all going to be all right; everything is going to be all right." ...we have to deny ourselves as we follow our master, Jesus, until we are wholly cleansed. . . .

But I did not see sin. I believe it has no substance or real existence. It can only be known by the pain it causes....It purges us and makes us know ourselves, so that we ask for mercy. ...Christ has compassion upon us because of our sin. . . .so now I was filled with compassion for all my fellow Christians. . . .For Holy Church shall be shaken at the world's sorrow, anguish, and tribulation, just as men shake a cloth in the wind. . . .He wants us to know that all this will be changed into glory and profit through his passion; to know, moreover, that we do not suffer on our own, but with him; to see in him the ground of our being. . . .To see this will stop us moaning and despairing about our own sufferings. We can see that our sin well deserves it, but that his love excuses us. . . .while I understood all this I was still troubled and grieved....Our Lord answered most humbly and cheerfully, showing me that the greatest wrong ever done was Adam's sin. . . .The meaning of our blessed Lord was this, "Since I have now made the greatest wrong good, I want you to know by this that I shall make good all wrongs of whatever degree" (Chapters 27, 28, 29).

In bringing us to the point where she shared something of her vision of the glory that is to be revealed, Julian has given us a complete outline of the Christian journey. Or so it seems. True enough, we have been instructed in the great mystery of the Trinity at work in our world; we have been shown something of our own destiny. But the journey we are making is not merely a matter of gaining some useful instruction; nor is it a matter of simply moving from one place to another. The journey we are on in life's pilgrimage is as much a matter of making us people of a certain kind, as it is of getting us to a certain terminus.

Julian now confronts the problem of sin and evil in the world with great intensity. Yet she sees that her questioning is in some ways "foolish." We must take things as they are, not as they might have been or could have been. Sin does exist. She even goes so far as to say sin is "necessary," which is possibly a result of her meditation on Matthew 18:7: "It is necessary that temptations come, but woe to the man by whom temptation comes." We must take the reality of sin as a fact. There is evil about us and within us. But Julian places this fact in the light of the great and boundless mercy of God. All shall be well! This is perhaps one of Julian's most popular sayings. This is a "locution," that is, an experience of words expressed in her mind. In the original it is even more catching and attractive than in more modern renditions:

> *Synne is behouely,*
> *but all shalle be wele,*
> *and all shalle be wele,*
> *and alle maner of thynge shalle be wele.*

This is a most optimistic and hope-filled assertion. And in the meanwhile we have to "deny" ourselves and follow the way of Christ until we are "wholly cleansed."

Julian does not see sin; she rightly sees it as a negation, but she also rightly knows that it can be discerned in the pain it causes. We know that to the prodigal son it certainly was a cause of pain: His initial selfishness ("Give me...") resulted in alienation (he went into a "far country"); he then experienced a great need (he had squandered all his property). This soon gave way, it seems, to a deep sense of frustration, aridity, and emptiness (a "great famine arose" and he knew "great want"). Finally, it brought him to degradation; the son made in his father's image would "gladly have fed on the pods the swine ate."

The parable of the prodigal makes us confront several pains of sin: the selfishness, the alienation, the need, the frustration, and the degradation. These aspects are the dynamic of sin, and they eat into our personalities. But our sins also contribute to these pains in others. None of us sins simply as an individual. And likewise these pains of sin often touch us, although they may be the effects of the sins of others or of society.

The Christian needs to be very sure about these various "pains" that sin causes. Whatever the kind of sin,the pains come and they disfigure the image and likeness of God, and distort the human's true role as child and sacrament of God on earth.

Just as the prodigal "came to his senses," so Julian sees that sin "purges us, and makes us know ourselves." We know ourselves as selfish people; each and all of us are touched by the "Give me" attitude of the prodigal; each of us has in some ways opted for alienation; each one of us feels a deep need and has been touched in some way by frustration and degradation. We need to ponder these pains. They are not merely indicators of our present state, they are also pointers to our future glory. The wounds of Jesus were the signs of his victory; to doubting Thomas they were the signs of the reality of resurrection and victory. In the same way, our wounds, the pains caused by sin, will be turned to glory. The power of God at work in Christ's victory over death is sufficient to change these pains of ours into victory.

Meanwhile, Julian has compassion for her fellows, that is, for all Christians who form the body of holy church, which is "shaken" as people shake a cloth in the wind. This is a very colorful image of Julian's to describe the suffering of the whole body of Christians, yet one can also imagine the shaking being a cleansing and refreshing thing.

Despite the clarity of the answer, Julian is still distressed "troubled and grieved" (Chapter 29). We know it is not enough to have a "solution"; our faith is not merely a matter of being given suitably convincing arguments and reasons, though they doubtless help. We sometimes have to learn to stay with the mystery, to live with the tension, and bear the burden of our pain. Healing is not instantaneous, nor is growth. Julian had to learn to live through the tensions of faith.

So Julian reminds us that our experience of God is not simply an academic, intellectual thing. It is something that must be learned through our own pain and confusion. This pain and effort teaches us our own fragility, and our fragility is the means God uses to teach us about the divine mercy, healing power, and creative purposes for us.

CHAPTER 15

God Revealing and Concealing

He gave me to understand that (something) is clear, beautiful, splendid, and abundant. ...To it we are bound, and to it we are drawn by God; in it we are advised, and in it we are instructed, inwardly by the Holy Spirit, and outwardly through the same grace by Holy Church. In this our Lord intends us to be occupied: delighted in himself, as he delights in us....

(But there is also something) completely hidden from us, for it deals with all those things that do not concern our salvation. It is our Lord's own private matter. . . .

Here it was that I was taught to trust and rejoice only in our blessed Saviour Jesus, and in whatever circumstances. . . .

God wills that we be enfolded—in rest and peace...This is his thirst: his love and longing for us that goes on enduring until we see the Day of Judgement. ...We are not as fully whole in him now as we shall be then. . . .

(Yet) we see deeds done that are so evil, and inju-

ries inflicted that are so great, that it seems impossible that any good can come of them....There still remains a deed which the blessed Trinity will do at the last Day...yet when and how it will be done is unknown. . . .

Be content whether he conceals or reveals (Chapters 30, 31, 32, 33).

As one re-reads the longer text it is clear that Julian has to spend much time pondering the things that challenged her. There were no instant solutions; the revelations she experienced all needed time and pain and living before they came to a real experience of Christian peace.

In Chapter 30 and the following Julian confronts the problem of the interplay of light and darkness in our lives. There are some things we can see and in some sense grasp, but there are also mysteries; many things are shrouded in darkness.

Some things are "clear, beautiful, splendid, and abundant." With St. John each of us can say, "We have seen his glory" (1:14). Julian sees that this is so inwardly through the teaching of the Holy Spirit and outwardly through the teaching of the church. At once she affirms that we have a great deal of light; we are given much to help us on our way. This light comes through the inward working of the Holy Spirit (that is, in our own prayer life) and also through the teaching of holy church (that is, through its full life of Scriptures, creed, and worship).

It is doubtless easy to take all this for granted; some part of our prayer should be to focus on the great truths we live. To many people the faith seems a complicated thing, a great mass of duties and details. For many people it is very difficult to see the basic central truths separate from the less important aspects that must necessarily become intertwined with them throughout the course of time.

In and through Jesus Christ, who was a man like us in all but sin, our impoverished and broken humanity is brought into a healing and living contact with the God who is both transcendent and immanent. Our living of this mystery of the Trinity is always basic and fundamental in our faith and it is facilitated and affected by our being enlightened by the Scriptures and by our meeting with Christ in the sacraments. All this is deeply personal. Like Mary, who symbolizes the faith of every Christian, we can say our "fiat." But it is equally communal, for it takes place within a faith community, the church.

It is only in this Christian family that we can reach the full stature of our humanity and be at home in the eternal.

All these great truths are our "light"; we need to nurture and nourish them in prayer. But as well as being bathed in all this light, we are also surrounded by darkness. As Julian has it, there are things that are "completely hidden" and demand of us a firm trust in the goodness of God:

> Even though I walk through the
> valley of the shadow of death,
> I fear no evil:
> for you are with me (Psalm 23:3).

Even though the darkness is not dark to God and the night is as clear as day (Psalm 139:12), to us who walk in it, it is still darkness, a very real part of our experience. For each one of us there is the darkness of our future: We do not know what our character or condition will be in the future or at the end time. There is also the darkness of our past: There is the vast hinterland of our subconscious that has stored and only dimly remembers experiences, and there are legacies from our collective past as members of a family and a people. There is even the mystery of the present: We can hardly guess at the full impact of our thoughts and actions on those about us, or indeed, their influence upon ourselves. Each of us is a mystery to oneself, and therefore each of us faces the "hidden" in ourselves, and in our environment. Some of these are secrets because God wills it so; others because of our sinfulness. We are "blind and ignorant" (Chapter 34).

There are some things Julian would like to know. She was anxious to see something of hell and purgatory, but this was not granted her (Chapter 33) and she was anxious to discover whether a friend would faithfully persevere (Chapter 35) and to this "I received no reply whatever." Julian is learning to live with the apparent contradictions and tensions that a faith-life involves. She is prepared to face the pain involved in those deeds which are so obviously evil that one wonders how any good can come from them. Yet she also believes that there remains a great deed that the Trinity will do at the last day. No matter how great the evil, the goodness of God is greater; no matter how mysterious the darkness, the light will not be overcome; the pain will be as nothing compared to the joy. Throughout the darkness we remember the cry of the Crucified one: "I thirst" (John 19:28). God is seeking us.

Walking in these tensions is one way of viewing our growth. We are still not "fully whole," as Julian so rightly remarks. We are still being shaped and made, still becoming the sort of men and women God desires us to be, still being discovered and found. And so Julian completes this view with another of her great syntheses. Just as seeking is as good as seeing (Chapter 10), and "weal and woe" are both equally his love (Chapter 15), and as suffering is being changed to glory because God is the ground of our being (Chapter 28), so here we must be

content whether he conceals or reveals.

And this takes us back to the image of the Blessed Trinity enfolding us in love. We are enfolded in rest and peace. The painful process of learning to live with the tension between the darkness and the light, the concealing and revealing, is also the gradual growth of the one tangible legacy Christ has promised us: his peace.

St. Teresa also knew that peace was possible in the midst of the pain and darkness:

> Let nothing disturb thee,
> Let nothing dismay thee,
> All things pass,
> God never changes.

CHAPTER 16

Learning Compunction and Contrition

While we live, whenever in our folly we turn to contemplate what is forbidden, our Lord God, in his blessed tenderness, with a touch calls us, speaking in our soul. "Let go what you are loving, dearest child. Mean me. I am all you want...."

So we humble ourselves, and fear God, crying for his help and grace. Miracles follow; and they come through the supreme power, wisdom, and goodness of God. . . .Thus our faith is strengthened, and our hope increased in love. . . .

God reminded me that I would sin...."I" here stands for all. Because of this I began to be rather fearful. And our Lord answered, "I am keeping you very securely...."

there is a godly will in (us). . . .Our primary concern is to see that our love does not fail.

Sin...is the scourge which so reduces a man or woman and makes him loathsome in his own sight...until the touch of the Holy Spirit forces him to contrition, and turns his bitterness to the hope

*of God's mercy. Then he begins to heal his
wounds, and to rouse his soul as it turns to the life
of Holy Church. The Holy Spirit leads him on to
confession. . . .Because of the humility we acquire
this way we are exalted in the sight of God by his
grace, and know a very deep contrition and compassion and a genuine longing for God. . . .*

*Our failing does not stop his loving us. Peace and
love are always at work in us, but we are not always in peace and love...(Chapters 36, 37, 39).*

As we make our journey Godward we are frequently challenged by our sinfulness. Even when we are apparently
confident of the love of God and take some joy in his presence and gifts, we can still turn to "contemplate what is
forbidden." This, to Julian, is sheer foolishness. Such, too,
was clearly the lot of the prodigal son until he came to his
senses. But in these moments we are not left alone or ne-
glected. Julian speaks of the Lord's blessed tenderness in
touching us and speaking to us. St. Augustine expressed
much the same thought in the *Confessions* (VI:5): "O Lord,
you laid your most gentle, most merciful finger upon my
heart and set my thoughts in order."

With Augustine, the folly had been both a false way of
acting and a false way of believing. In the midst of our folly
the Lord touches us and gives us the grace of compunction. In Chapter 35 Julian gives us her understanding of
the doctrine of compunction: the grace of God that moves
the heart to recognize the folly of its sin and indeed the
possibility of future failures, and also stirs the heart to seek
God. It is the movement of the prodigal when he sets off
again toward his father's house, after his thoughts had
been set in order, after he had come to his senses.

In Chapter 37 Julian turns her attention to the Father.
The Lord said, "I am keeping you very securely." We are

reminded of the psalmist, expressing sentiments suitable for an exile:

> The Lord will keep you from all evil; he will keep
>   your life.
> The Lord will keep your going out and your com-
>   ing in from this time forth and for evermore
> (Psalm 120:7-8).

These words remind us that God continues to love and to keep us even when in our folly we turn to what is self-destructive. William Law in *The Spirit of Love* remarks that "every action and notion of self has the spirit of Antichrist and murders the divine life within you." Despite this power of self-destruction, God continues to love us. "But thou, our God, are kind and true, patient, and ruling all things in mercy. For even if we sin we are thine, knowing thy power" (Wisdom 15:1).

Even in our sin we remain creatures of God; we are still his image and likeness, though the reflection of God in our actions is sadly blurred; we are still children of God and members of his household, though we stray. Julian is very clear that even in our sin there is something godly that remains: "a godly will that has never consented to sin." Something good and loveable remains. Yet we still have to face the reality of our erring free will. Although God's love does not fail, we have to make every effort to see that "our love does not fail."

And while we admit the continuing love of God for the sinner, we are also sure that Julian is right in asserting that the "scourge" of sin makes us "loathsome" in our own sight. Augustine in *Confessions* (II:2) expresses it in much stronger language:

> Nor did I escape your scourges. No mortal can.
> You were always by me, mercifully hard upon
> me, and besprinkling all my illicit pleasures with
> certain elements of bitterness, to draw me on to
> seek for pleasures in which no bitterness should

be. And where was I to find such pleasures save in you, O Lord, You who use sorrow to teach, and wound to heal, and kill us lest we die to you.

This sense of compunction leads on to contrition; this is sought in the life of the church, the sacrament of God's healing presence in the world. Throughout Julian's writings there are frequent references to the life of the church. The notion is often propounded that the great mystics are so individualistic as to be more or less in opposition to the visible church. Nothing could be further from the truth in Julian's case, as in the case of the other great spiritual authors. The deeply personal and the sacramental are held in a wise balance and tension.

In compunction, contrition, and then in sacramental reconciliation we are taught to face our own sinfulness and to accept it as a reality. But Julian is right in finding it a difficult thing to accept; it can only leave us "loathsome" in our own sight. But we learn the truth about ourselves. This teaches us humility; it is part of the process of knowing ourselves. But at the same time our faith teaches that the sinner, while unaccepable to self, is acceptable to God. This again is a cause of tension. It is another of those ambivalent or apparently contradictory stances the faith demands. And it occasions yet another of those wonderfully harmonizing statements from Julian. We who have now been taught that seeking is as good as seeing, that weal or woe are both equally his love, are now taught that

Peace and love are always at work in us, but we are not always in peace or love.

We have managed to wander far from God in our sinfulness, but God has not deserted us.

Living through this tension is a necessary part of the Christian's growth in self-acceptance. In this we know ourselves to be unacceptable to ourselves in so many ways, but we also learn to know that we are acceptable to God. In these chapters Julian also gives her teaching on the preparation for prayer. We always come to our prayer as people who are broken and in need of mercy, but also as people who know that mercy is available. The Father always welcomes us. We have been found and restored to life.

And so in our prayer we come to face yet another tension of faith: our being unacceptable to ourselves yet acceptable to God. Learning to live with this tension is yet another means whereby God gives us the gift of peace, which is beyond all understanding. And so often in our prayer we come before God not merely as people in need, but also as people with one or other aspect of this tension of faith. We stand before the Mystery and this in itself is a cleansing and healing experience. As the author of the *Cloud of Unknowing* puts it so sharply and clearly:

> So if you are to stand and not fall, never give up your firm intention: beat away at this cloud of unknowing between you and God with that sharp dart of longing love. Hate to think about anything less than God, and let nothing whatever distract you from this purpose. It is only thus that you can destroy the ground and root of sin.

So at some stage in our prayer we learn to recognize frankly both our dissatisfaction with self and also God's abiding love for us. In this tension we simply stand before God; we are in need of healing, he is full of mercy and compassion. Our desire so to stand is a sign of the "godly will" that does not sin; it is the thin thread of gold that is harbinger of final and full healing. In the quietness of this prayer we grow less and less, and godliness increases; the selfishness of sin is slowly turned toward God; the cancer of our sinfulness is slowly burned out by the rays of God's love.

And toward the end of Chapter 40 Julian affirms:

> *The same blessed love teaches us that we should hate sin for Love's sake alone. I am quite clear about this: the more a soul sees this in the courtesy*

*and love of our Lord God, the more he hates to sin,
and the greater is his sense of shame. . . .When we
set our will to be loving and humble the effect of
mercy and grace is to make everyone beautiful and
clean.*

CHAPTER 17

Union with God

(The Fourteenth Revelation)

Our Lord showed me about prayer. . . .I now see that there are two conditions about prayer. One concerns its rightness, the other our sure trust.

Often our trust is not wholehearted, for we are not sure that God hears us. We think it is due to our unworthiness and because we feel absolutely nothing: we are often as barren and dry after our prayers as before. . . .All this our Lord brought immediately to mind, and in this revelation said, "I am the foundation of your praying. In the first place my will is that you should pray, and then I make it your will too, and since it is I who make you pray, and you do so pray, how can you not have what you ask for?"...for it is quite impossible that we should pray for mercy and grace, and not receive it!

Prayer is full of grace, and lasting, for it is united with and fixed into the will of our Lord by the inner working of the Holy Spirit. . . .

Our Lord is greatly cheered by our prayer. He looks for it, and he wants it. . . .So he says, "Pray inward-

*ly, even if you do not enjoy it. It does you good,
though you feel nothing, see nothing. Yes, even
though you think you are doing nothing. For
when you are dry, empty, sick, or weak, at such a
time is your prayer most pleasing to me. . . ."*

*We should know what is the outcome and pur-
pose of our prayers, namely, that we should be
united with our Lord and like him in every
thing....*

Here we are to stand and stay.

*Our whole strength and aim is set on beholding
(Chapters 41, 42, 43).*

Julian now confronts another aspect of the ambivalence
that is part of our human condition and revealed in our
prayer. There is much about prayer that is good and right.
It is the will of the Lord that we pray. But on the other
hand there is the unmasking of human weakness in the
course of prayer. We very often don't enjoy it; we feel so
"dry, empty, sick and weak."

Thus Julian looks at the tension between what we believe God is doing in prayer and our own fickle feelings.
She is very sure that we must have great trust in what God
is doing. And here she shows (and so often) her vigorous
mental capacity. There are sound arguments supporting
the reality of God in prayer: God wills our prayer, preven-
ient grace moves us to pray, and Julian is sure that we receive the necessary blessings for which we pray. In other
words, we have been given the gift of prayer. So often it
seems to us that *we* pray; *we* make the effort to attend,
think, love and discern our next few steps along the pilgrim way. But the basic truth about prayer is far different.
Fr. Andre Louf in *Teach Us to Pray* reminds us that whatever we may see as *our* part, our effort, prayer is still fun-
damentally a gift:

For our heart is already in a *state of prayer*. We received prayer along with grace, in our baptism....in the profound depth of the self, we have a continuing contact with God. God's Holy Spirit has taken us over, has assumed complete possession of us; he has become the breath of our breath and spirit of our spirit.

Throughout her work, especially in the later chapters, Julian speaks often of the Holy Spirit, and speaks in particular of the "inner working" of the Holy Spirit (v.g. Chapters 39, 41, 80). This indwelling of the Spirit is the foundation of our praying.

In a sermon entitled "The Indwelling Spirit" Newman said:

The Holy Ghost...dwells in body and soul, as in a temple...he pervades us (if it may so be said) as light pervades a building, or as a sweet perfume the folds of some honourable robe; so that, in Scripture language, we are said to be in him, and he in us. . . .It is plain that such an inhabitation brings the Christian into a state altogether new and marvellous.

This indwelling of the Spirit makes us "fixed into the will of our Lord." This, despite the human feelings that persist, there can be a real prayer of union with God. This inner working of the Holy Spirit is what prompts us to pray for the essentials: "mercy and grace." That is for God. This is the same sort of petition repeatedly urged by the author of *The Cloud*: "mean God and not what you get out of him." This prayer also includes gratitude. Julian says, "Thanksgiving is a real, interior, knowledge." Thus prayer of deep union with God includes both petition and thanksgiving.

While this whole world of mystery is taking place in our inner selves, we can have an outer layer of being, a shell as it were, that seems "dry, empty, sick or weak."

In her prayer Julian is moving toward a greater synthesis. The dichotomy still persists (and will continue to persist). The Spirit of all truth touches the life that is limited and barren; the Spirit of love touches the life that is so heavy and lethargic. The attitude to adopt, indeed the only possible stance to take, is one of complete passivity and docility before the Spirit, even to the point where it seems that we are feeling, seeing, and doing nothing.

Thus we move to the stage where, accepting the complexing and confusing array of emotional responses we are capable of producing, we simply stand passive before God. We must make our own the words of the psalmist: "Be still and know that I am God" (Psalm 45). Thus "our whole strength and aim is set on beholding." We stand passive before God, even if our beholding is simply beholding the cloud of unknowing. The solution to the human dichotomy this time is not so much an intellectual insight or telling epigram. It is simply that we stay with the mystery:

Here we are to stand and stay (Chapter 42).

As we remain faithful to our life of prayer, we need to remember that it has all been made possible by God. There is not simply a human element that is acutely conscious of its frailty and imperfection, and a divine component that is love enveloped in mystery. The divine has touched the human. The very fact of our striving to pray is itself an answer to prayer. God is slowly turning our broken humanity toward himself.

I am sure that no one genuinely asks for mercy and grace without mercy and grace having been given him first (Chapter 42).

In a wonderfully concise Chapter (44) Julian shows us that this is nothing but being enfolded in the life of the Trinity. She now moves to a deeper appreciation of the meaning of the first revelation and "that wonderful example of the action of truth and wisdom in the soul of our Blessed Lady":

Truth sees God: wisdom gazes on God. And these two produce a third, a holy wondering delight in God, which is love. Where there is indeed truth and wisdom, there too is love, springing from them both. And all of God's making: for he is eternal sovereign truth, eternal sovereign wisdom, eternal sovereign love, uncreated (Chapter 44).

As we consciously battle with our inertia and our apparent inability to pray, we need to be reminded of the wider context in which we pray, and the gift of prayer that is ours; it is nothing other than the life of the Trinity. Julian is all too well aware that we are self-conscious beings, overly aware of our fragile and confused selves and so little aware of the God in whom we live and move.

So we come to know that we have this great treasure in earthen vessels (2 Corinthians 4:7).

CHAPTER 18

Knowing Self

God judges us according to our essential nature, which is forever kept whole, safe and sound in him. . . .But man judges according to his changeable feelings, which are now this, now that, and which vary with his particular mood, and display themselves outwardly. Man's judgement is confused, inconsistent: sometimes it is good and tolerant, sometimes it is harsh and difficult. When it is good and tolerant it is part of God's righteousness, and when it is harsh and difficult our good Lord reforms it by the action of that mercy and grace which are the result of his blessed passion.

Our fleeting life here, with its physical senses, does not know what our real self is, but in that Day we will see it truly and clearly. . . .we shall never wholly know our self until the very last moment, when this passing life with its pain and woe shall come to its end. . . .

Man is fickle in this life, and by his frailty and ignorance falls into sin. He is essentially weak and foolish, and his will can be overborne. In his lifetime he experiences storms, sorrows and grief; and the reason is that he is blind: he does not see god. . . .

But our good Lord, the Holy Spirit, who is ever-lasting life and who securely dwells in our soul, keeps us, and by his grace produces a real peace, Godlike and docile. In this merciful fashion our Lord is always leading us amidst the changes and chances of this mortal life.

We cannot be safe and happy until we know real love and peace: that is what salvation is. . . .there will be no joyful salvation or eternal happiness until we are completely at peace and in love. In other words, until we are wholly content with God...in love and at peace with ourselves, our fellow Christians and with all that God loves (Chapters 45, 46, 47, 48, 49).

As in our last section, so here Julian brings us back to the apparent ambivalence of our human situation. On the one hand there is the being of God that underpins and supports all; it is the strong hand clasping the fragile hazelnut; it is a loving presence that keeps us "whole, safe and sound." On the other hand, we are confronted with our own fickle nature: sometimes confused and inconsistent and at other times good and tolerant. But here too, there is a ray of hope. When we humans are at our best we are a reflection of the goodness of God, a sacrament of the divine. And even our less loveable qualities are a being slowly re-formed and made wholesome.

So some part of our prayer is a challenge to grow in self-knowledge: to know ourselves as both something good and acceptable and an image (however faint) of the goodness of God. In a celebrated passage the author of the *Cloud of Unknowing* tells us to "strain every nerve in every possible way to know and experience yourself as you really are. It will not be long, I suspect, before you have a real knowledge and experience of God as he is "(Chapter 14). This, the author explains, is humility, which "is nothing else but a true knowledge and awareness of oneself as one really is" (Chapter 13).

This sort of self-knowledge for the man or woman of prayer is an acknowledgment of the goodness in ourselves, which is a clear indication of the presence of God, but it is also an acknowledgment of our limitations, shortcomings, and failings. These also are being touched by the Maker, Keeper, and Lover. We are being slowly refashioned in the image of Christ, the perfect one.

The parable of the sower (Mark 4) gives us some hint how we can accept the strange mixture of good and evil in ourselves. Each one of us is like the field: Some part of it is good soil (for which we must be thankful), some part of it is like rocky ground (which calls for the hard heart to be replaced by a heart of flesh), some part of it is disfigured by thorns (the distractions and ungodly interests that limit our harvest of good and must be painfully and patiently eradicated), and some part of it is like a pathway (those aspects of our personalities hardened into habitual ways of acting). It will take the sower many a sowing and plowing (and in Palestine the plowing followed the sowing) to bring that mixed bag of a field into a fully productive one. We need much patience with ourselves and with the sower.

Walter Hilton in *The Ladder of Perfection* has given us a very wonderful approach to this problem of gradual conversion through life. He distinguishes between two types of reformation:

> As I said previously, this reformation in faith can be achieved quite easily. Reformation in faith and feeling must follow; this is not so easily attained, and comes only after patient and prolonged effort. For all God's chosen are reformed in faith, although they may still remain in the lowest degree of charity; but reformation in feeling comes only to souls who reach a state of perfection, and it cannot be achieved all at once. A soul can reach it only through great grace and by

prolonged spiritual effort, but it must first be healed of its spiritual sickness. Its bitter passions, bodily desires, and unregenerate feelings have to be burned out of the heart by the fire of desire, and new feelings of burning love and spiritual light have to be infused by grace.

We have already been "re-formed" in faith: Our baptism and the grace of the sacraments and the godly influences in our lives all do something to us. But it takes a lengthy time for our "feelings" to come into harmony and unity with this grace given.

In these chapters Julian is grappling with the mystery of our being sinful creatures, yet still in the hands of God's loving care. Julian could not see "blame or wrath" in God (Chapter 45) and she could see no anger except on the human part (Chapter 48). However, she looks forward to the parable of the lord and his servant in which some light is shed on the problem. There is the "blame of sin which has been hanging over us" and yet God regards us with "no more blame than if we had been as pure and holy as his angels in heaven" (Chapter 50). But our whole life is "grounded and rooted in love" (Chapter 49).

However, Julian is not merely searching for a theoretical answer to her problem; nor does she imagine that knowledge alone can solve the mystery. Hers is a very experiential approach. She has made an effort to understand her own complexity of feelings and human responses, and she seeks to see the mercy of God leading her to her fullness of life. The loving mercy of God enables this healing transformation to take place. Julian's writing prompts us to look realistically at ourselves to see the merciful hand of God leading us forward. We all need to confront ourselves in a realistic and truthful manner and to be able to make our own the promise given Paul:"My grace is sufficient for you for my power is made perfect in weakness" (1 Corinthians 12:9).

Confronting our own weakness is no easy matter. We

can often employ subtle or violent means to prevent our having to face it. It is all too easy to be angry and blame others, to indulge in frenzied activity and avoid having to face ourselves, to dismiss the views of others as misunderstandings and prejudice. Perhaps we can only come to really know ourselves through time spent in prayer over a considerable span of time. The Spirit of peace is slowly revealing us to ourselves, and slowly producing a real peace that is docile: willing to learn and to change.

This mystery of self is not an easy one to face. We need patience with ourselves and with God if we are to accept both the fickle, feeble self, and also the goodness of God within ourselves. Faith enables us to hold these two in a productive tension. It is productive because as we persevere with it, we learn to accept more and more "reality" and come to experience the peace of God.

CHAPTER 19

Lord and Servant

The lord is sitting down quietly, relaxed and peaceful: The servant is standing by his lord, humble and ready to do his bidding. And then I saw the lord look at his servant with rare love and tenderness, and quietly send him to a certain place to fulfil his purpose. Not only does that servant go, but he starts off at once, running with all speed, in his love to do what his master wanted. And without warning he falls headlong into a deep ditch, and injures himself very badly. And though he groans and moans and cries and struggles he is quite unable to get up or help himself in any way. To crown all, he could get no relief of any sort: he could not even turn his head to look at the lord who loved him, and who was so close to him. . . .

His pain was sevenfold...severe bruising...the sheer weight of his body...consequent weakness...his mind was shocked...he could not get up...he was quite alone...and lastly there was the hard rough surface on to which he had fallen....

Basically it was his own good will and great longing that had caused his fall....And it is thus that his master always sees him.

> *The natural consequences of (the Lord's) great goodness and worth was that his much beloved servant should be truly and gladly rewarded beyond anything he could have had had he not fallen. Yes, indeed, further; his fall and subsequent suffering were to be transformed into great and superlative honour and everlasting joy (Chapter 51).*

As we have seen, Julian believes sin exists; she is sure of that and accepts the teaching of the church in that respect. Yet she herself can see no anger in God, even though "sinners sometimes deserve God's blame and wrath" (Chapter 45). This baffles Julian, and she is anxious to find an answer. She has already indicated that the answer will be found in the "wonderful illustration of a lord and his servant." It is obvious that this illustration only slowly came into proper focus, and is the fruit of many years of thought and prayer.

One might well regard this illustration as the centerpiece of Julian's spiritual teaching. It is a very "medieval" piece of writing. It shows the medievalist's wonderful powers of memory and imagination. Every tiny detail seems to fit together to make something like a huge stained-glass window; every posture, color, and gesture seems to bear a weight of meaning.

So Julian solves her dilemma by a story and an image, rather than by a detailed piece of abstract reasoning. Perhaps that is the only way to speak religious truths that cannot be adequately tied down to words and concepts. The image and the story allow the meaning to reach beyond what we can immediately comprehend and hint at the mystery that is involved in our Christian living.

Such at any rate is the usual approach of the Lord himself. We are not given detailed theological descriptions of the Kingdom he came to found but are told that it is like a grain of mustard seed...leaven...a treasure hidden in a field...a merchant in search of fine pearls...a net thrown into the sea. The parables of the Lord give us hints and suggestions but do not encase the truth in an intellectual or verbal museum. The truths are greater than the words that express them, though the words give us reliable knowledge of those truths.

In this illustration of the lord and his servant, Julian tells us a great deal about her understanding of the mystery of God, the brokenness of humanity, and Christ's saving work. The lord is "sitting down quietly, relaxed and peaceful." This clearly reiterates Julian's teaching that there is no anger in God; he is in command, totally at peace. The servant is standing; that is, he is ready to do the lord's bidding. The fall he experiences clearly alters *his* condition, not the lord's. Then Julian describes the sad state of the fallen one: "To crown all" he had even lost sight of the lord who was still close to him and still loved him. Julian's seven-fold description of the fall is again a typically medieval device—the mystical number seven emphasizes the mystery and magnitude of the fall. But this is not merely a medieval fad. Julian's words help us to understand so much of what our sinfulness really means.

Despite this, the peace and love of God never waver. As for the servant, his fall was not a total destruction, nor a complete loss. Julian's teaching also echoes the traditional teaching of the church that redemption in Christ will more than compensate for the loss. Thus the church prays in the Easter Vigil (after the First Reading).

> Almighty and eternal God,
>> you created all things in wonderful beauty and
>> order.
> Help us now to perceive
>> how still more wonderful is the new creation
>> by which in the fullness of time
>> you redeemed your people
>> through the sacrifice of our passover, Jesus
>> Christ, who lives and reigns for ever.

Perhaps one of Julian's most significant points in this chapter is the admission that despite the seeming clarity and beauty of the illustration she was still baffled. There was much that could not apply to Adam as she had heard the story of the fall: "So there I had to leave it." It was only after nearly twenty years that she received the inner enlightenment to unravel the meaning.

Doubtless we can place too much emphasis on our intellectual understanding of the faith. We might do well to learn something of Julian's approach. She remained with the image, the story, and the illustration for nearly twenty years. Again we see her emphasis on the need for perseverance, regularity, and diligence in our prayer. All the while the power of the image was touching her mind and heart. Our faith is not merely something we must search to understand, and in which we must grow in a progressive, scientific manner. It is rather a power that is being exercised over us, and a capacity given to us. The Jews of old were taught by the constant yearly repetition of the great story of salvation; the old images were revived and re-lived. The church in her worship takes us through the same story, now completed in Christ. We do well to let these images speak to us, move us, and encourage us. As Christopher Bryant has written in *Jung and the Christian Way:*

> The study of the Bible might be transformed if we could understand the biblical images, not as poetical ways of stating what could with greater precision be stated in exact prose, but rather as powerful symbols able to release a flow of spiritual life in us, if only we will take them seriously and through imaginative reflection open ourselves to their impact.

God has provided us with images that are such symbols and can release a flow of spiritual life in us, if only we give prolonged attention to them, and in a real sense "contemplate" them. God has also given us powers of imagination that can enable us to construct and hold such images. It is a part of our prayer that is basic and on-going.

Such a fidelity to the image enabled Julian to see further, to deepen her appreciation of God and of what it means to be a Christian, to have one's life hidden with Christ in God. She goes on to tell us:

> *The lord who was sitting in solemn state, quietly and peacefully, I took to be God. The servant who stood before his lord I understood to be Adam. There was shown at that time just one man and his fall; to make us understand that God sees Everyman and his fall. In the sight of God everyman is one man, and one man is everyman. This man's strength was injured, and he was much weakened. His senses too were confused, for he turned away from looking at his lord. However, his will was still sound in God's sight, for I saw that our Lord commended and approved his will. But he was prevented from seeing this about his will, and therefore was in great sorrow and distress. He could not see clearly his loving lord, so gentle and kind towards him, nor could he see how he really stood in the eyes of that same loving master (Chapter 51).*

Here Julian's image takes on an even more profound significance: The servant has a twofold meaning, both the Everyman and the Christ. The two Adams had in some sense merged into the one. Christ has taken on our human brokenness and identified with it. Here is the suffering servant of Isaiah 53, the one despised and rejected, a man of sorrows and grief, the one who carries our griefs and sorrows, who was wounded for our transgressions and bruised for our iniquities.

Though Julian is still a beginner, she displays a wonderful wisdom:

> *At this time I began to learn how it is that God can still behold us in our sin. I went on to see that it is*

only pain that blames and punishes, but that our
gracious Lord comforts and sympathises, for he is
ever kindly disposed towards our soul, and, loving
us, longs to bring us to his bliss (Chapter 51).

The warmth and homeliness of her illustration of the lord
and the servant enable Julian to hold the truths in some
peaceful tension. There is human sin; it has done much to
weaken and break us. But there is the abiding love of God
who sees his son identified with imperfect humanity.

This great truth is suited to our needs:

Man in this life is blind and cannot see God, our
Father, as he is. Ans whenever he wills of his
goodness to show himself to man, he shows him-
self in great simplicity, as man (Chapter 51).

And because, as she so aptly states, Christ "is the true
Adam," this is also a truth about ourselves. At the end of
the story the servant is with the Lord, his Father, "crowned
with priceless splendour." This also involves us:

We are his crown, the crown which is the Father's
joy, the Son's honour, the Holy Spirit's pleasure
(Chapter 51).

CHAPTER 20

Marvelous Mix-up

Kept secure by Christ we are assured, by his touch of grace, of salvation; broken by Adam's fall, and in many ways by our own sins and sorrows, we are so darkened and blinded that we can hardly find any comfort. But in our heart we abide in God, and confidently trust to his mercy and grace. . . .he opens the eye of our understanding so that we can see; sometimes it is less, sometimes more, according to our God-given ability to receive it. Now we are uplifted by the one; now we are allowed to fall into the other. And this fluctuating is so baffling that we are hard put to know where we stand. . . .

It certainly is a marvellous mix-up! (Chapter 52).

In his sermon on the ascension of our lord (in *Pastoral Sermons*) Ronald Knox speaks of the "nursery language of sight and sense [which] is only symbol, only metaphor," which we use to describe the ascension. And he goes on to say:

Whatever else is true, we know that a human nature, like ours and therefore representative of ours, has penetrated behind the last barrier, has crossed the last threshold, which separates the human from the divine. And because we are one in and with him, his achievement is ours; St. Paul does not hesitate to describe Christian people as here and now "enthroned above the heavens, in Christ Jesus." You and I, already enthroned in heaven; that is hard to believe, hard to understand.

Yet we believe it to be true, to be the reality in which we are. The parable of the lord and servant illustrates again the profound mystery of the human situation. We are with Christ who is already crowned in glory, and we are also continuing our earthly pilgrimage. As Julian says, we are "kept secure" yet we are "broken...darkened and blinded." These are the two sides to the human story. At one moment we seem to be more conscious of one aspect, and then the other comes more clearly into focus.

Now another note seems to enter Julian's understanding of our pilgrimage and she seems to display a deeper wisdom. The parable has enabled her to inject a deeper note of joy into her acceptance of the human situation: "It is all a marvellous mix-up." This seems to suggest something like a hearty, good-natured abandonment. Christ has identified with our weakness; he has entered our human story in a mysterious manner; the old and the new Adam have somehow merged. There is no cause for undue anxiety, no rushing into panic. It is quite certain that everything is held in God's loving providence, even if it is not always clearly seen or felt by us.

Psychologists have attempted to understand something of our human complexity. We all have areas of mystery and elements of darkness and shadow. We need to remember that none of this is outside the loving providence of God. It is all touched by the one who saves and heals; it is all being enlivened by the one who loves, all being created whole and entire by the one who creates. Maker, Keeper, and Lover have the whole bewildering fluctuation in hand. The healing process takes time. It has to be achieved through a series of experiences. It is known not so much as knowledge but as a deepening and profound wisdom. So we learn to trust, in quietness and in confidence—and with good humor. Religion does not have to be dour.

CHAPTER 21

God as Mother

So Jesus Christ who sets good against evil is our real Mother. We owe our being to him—and this is the essence of motherhood!—and all the delightful, loving protection which ever follows. God is as really our Mother as he is our Father. . . .

The human mother will suckle her child with her own milk, but our beloved Mother, Jesus, feeds us with himself, and, with the most tender courtesy, does it by means of the Blessed Sacrament, the precious food of all true life. And he keeps us going through his mercy and grace by all the sacraments. This is what he meant when he said, "It is I whom Holy Church preaches and teaches." In other words, "All the health and life of sacraments, all the virtue and grace of my word, all the goodness laid up for you in Holy Church—it is I" (Chapters 59, 60).

Julian has already prepared us for the idea of God as mother. In Chapter 48 she referred to "Mercy (being) compassionate with the tender love of motherhood"; in Chapter 52 she reminded us that no one word is capable of stating all we would want to say about God. She saw him "rejoicing to be our Father; rejoicing too to be our Mother...Husband (Isaiah 42:5)...Brother (Hebrews 2:17) and our Saviour." Julian's teaching on God as mother is not entirely original, although she does give it more emphasis than previous writers. This teaching has some foundations in biblical allusions. Isaiah refers to God's love being like a mother's: "As one whom his mother comforts, so I will comfort you; you shall be comforted in Jerusalem" (Isaiah 66:13).

In Matthew our Lord refers to his love as being like that of a mother hen for her brood (23:37). In Christian tradition, too, the idea has some place. St. Anselm, in his prayer to Paul (in which he likens Paul to a mother), speaks of Christ:

> And you, Jesus, are you not also a mother?
> Are you not the mother who, like a hen,
> gathers her chickens under her wings?
> Truly, Lord, you are a mother;
> for both they who are in labor
> and they who are brought forth
> are accepted by you.

The image in Matthew of the mother hen here seems to merge with another traditional Christian symbol, the pelican. The pelican was seen as a figure of Christ's motherly love in the Eucharist. The sixth stanza of the old medieval hymn *Adoro te* contained reference to the pelican feeding her young with her own blood. And the human mother suckles her young with her own milk.

The Eucharist then is the point where all these natural and biblical images coalesce. In Holy Communion we experience the "most tender courtesy of Christ" whose self-emptying and self-giving are the meaning of this "precious food of all true life." Here is "health and life," found only in Jesus, and it comes to us with the tenderness and warmth that Julian associates with the word "mother."

But Julian's appreciation of the Eucharist is not merely

as a deeply personal and individual contact with the Lord. It is that, but much more besides. It is also an ecclesial thing; it has a communal aspect. And here the two are intertwined in a way reminiscent of Augustine's adage that Jesus loves each one of us as though we were the only one and all of us as they we were the only one.

Julian's appreciation moves effortlessly from the personal to the communal; the spirituality of the individual exists in the totality of the Christian community, which is the church.

Chapter 60 closes with a typically lucid explanation: Julian discusses the manner in which a mother watches over and nurtures each stage of a child's growth. Christ watches over each stage of our growth, so it is clear to her that the word *mother* can be applied to him:

> *This fine and lovely word...cannot properly be used of any but him, and of her who is his own true Mother—and ours. In essence motherhood means love and kindness, wisdom, knowledge, goodness.*

Julian's ability to link the notion of motherhood with Eucharist can do much to deepen our appreciation of the Mystery we celebrate week by week. The mighty acts of God—the death, resurrection, and ascension of Christ, and the sending of the Spirit—come to us in a gentle, homely, and indeed "motherly" fashion. They are mighty deeds, but they come to us gently in simple things at the Eucharist. The great action of God is making us his people, but not in a dictatorial fashion or as a mass herding of people. The word of God is basically a homely and courteous thing. Julian is so right to see it so aptly summed up in "this fine and lovely word," mother.

CHAPTER 22

God and Church

And he wants us to copy the child who always and naturally trusts mother's love through thick and thin.

Moreover he wills that we should hold tight to the Faith of Holy Church, and find there in that Communion of Saints our dearest Mother, who comforts us because she really understands. Individuals may often break down—or so it seems to them—but the whole body of Holy Church is unbreakable, whether in the past, present, or future. So it is a good, sound, grace-bringing thing to resolve, humbly but firmly, to be fastened and united to Holy Church our Mother—in other words, to Jesus Christ. For the merciful ample flood of his precious blood and water suffices to make us sweet and clean; the Saviour's blessed wounds are open, and rejoice to heal us; the dear, gracious hands of our Mother are ever about us, and eager to help.

In all this work he functions as a kindly nurse who has no other business than to care for the wellbeing of her charge. It is his business to save us; it is his glory to do this for us; and it is his will that we should know it. For it is also his will that we

*should love him dearly, and trust him humbly
and wholeheartedly. All this he showed in those
gracious words, "I will keep you safe and sound"
(Chapter 61).*

Few Christians would have more cause for anxiety about
the church than Western Europeans during the late fourteenth century. The period presents a stark contrast to the
century following the Fourth Lateran Council (1215) when
the church enjoyed vigorous and confident leadership and
displayed such zeal and energy in fulfilling its mission. By
Julian's time this renewal movement was a spent force. In
England the whole tone of life seemed poorer. To add to the
malaise the country had its first major heretic in John Wycliffe; the Hundred Years War (1338-1453) was something of
a running sore; then the outbreak of the Black Death in
1348 cast a pall over European life that was to linger for
many generations. The destruction, fear, and gloom that
the plague occasioned formed that backdrop against which
one must read the history of the late fourteenth century.
And from 1378 to 1417 an already demoralized church and
society was to witness the scandal of the Great Western
Schism in which the church was divided against itself.

The historical background makes good sense of Julian's
earlier statement that the church will be shaken as "men
shake a cloth in the wind" (Chapter 28). Yet the many de-
pressing aspects of the human face of the church did not
blur Julian's appreciation of the deeper truths. The Christian of mature faith can both lament and accept the shortcomings of the church, and work with urgency to correct
the former, while having a deep peace deriving from the
greater meaning of the church. For the one who professes
to "believe" in the holy Catholic church, the unseen rather
than the seen engages the attention. And as St. Paul urges
us, we must keep our minds on what is unseen rather
than on what is seen. The church is the sacrament of sal-

vation; the saving power at work in it and through it is greater than the unpolished image it sometimes presents to the world. Julian had such a vision of the unseen.

Indeed, she makes it clear that this is a matter of faith and not sight; our acceptance of the reality of the church is a realization that we belong to a body larger than the earthly one we see. And here in this communion of saints we experience this fundamental acceptance by God. God is mother and the divine acceptance of us is ministered through this mother, the church. It is here that the saving grace of Jesus Christ is made available to us.

In this vision of faith our ambivalent attitudes to the church come to a harmony and peace. It is no surprising thing to find that the church is a less than perfect image of the grace it bears. That will always be the problem with sacraments; they can never fully portray the beauty they impart. At best they can only hint and suggest the realities they give us. So there is something understandable about comments such as that made by C.S. Lewis when he rediscovered his faith in Christ. He found the idea of a church unattractive, and humorously remarked that he would rather "join a zoo." But he soon came to see that church is necessary—it is Christ's body, the thing through which Christ acts.

When confronted with anxieties about the "state of the church" (and that means a bewildering variety of causes for complaint), the only thing most of us can do is try a little harder to make oneself, as part of that body of Christ, a little more like what the whole body should be: a vibrant sign of God's saving love in the midst of the world, a group of people struggling to realize the Kingdom already in our midst, a band of pilgrims straining forward to the promised homeland.

In this chapter, as in the preceding piece concerning the idea of God as mother, Julian continues to spell out the implications of the parable of the lord and servant. God cares for his people with a motherly love; that tender love is imparted through the church, Christ's body. Thus Julian challenges us to see beyond appearances and human defects to the beauty of God's love filtered through church and sacrament.

When we talk of "church" it is all too easy to be ensnared into seeing it as a political or social or even an economic reality. Of course, it is set firmly in this world of ours and is part of the human story. But it is also fixed into the unseen world and is part of the divine story of salvation. Once again, Julian invites us to hold these two aspects together in a faith-filled, quiet tension.

CHAPTER 23

Through the Course of Time

When we by God's mercy and help agree with nature and grace we shall see in very truth that sin is more vile and painful than hell itself. Indeed there is no comparison: sin contradicts our nature. For just as sin is really unclean, so it is really unnatural, and therefore is a horrible thing for the beloved soul to see when, taught by nature and grace, it would be beautiful and shining in the sight of God.

We have no fear of this, unless it is the kind of fear that urges us on. But we make our humble complaint to our beloved Mother, and he sprinkles us with his precious blood, and makes our soul pliable and tender, and restores us to our full beauty in course of time. This is his glory and our eternal joy. And this sweet and lovely work he will never cease from doing until all his beloved children are born and delivered. This was showed in the explanation of his spiritual thirst, that longing that loves and lasts until the Day of Judgement. . . .

I saw that God rewards man for his patience in waiting on God's will and God's time, and for extending that patience over the whole span of life (Chapters 63, 64).

Julian sees that sin is vile and unnatural and painful. To be sinful is to be something less than our true selves. Here Julian seems to be echoing the teaching of writers such as St. Bernard who taught that in Christ we are restored to our true selves. We only become fully and truly ourselves when we allow ourselves to be merged with Christ, as he has allowed himself to become one with us. Here we see the reverse side of the parable of the lord and servant: Christ has identified with fallen humanity; the second Adam merges with the first. This saving activity of God is a real mothering; his maternal love touches us in the sacramental life of the church. This saving work of God has its complement and counterpart in our movement away from sin. Our nature shrinks from what is vile, painful, and a denial of our true selves—or it should. But we know that the lure of sin still has a power to attract; it can still seem to us to be satisfying, liberating, and enjoyable. This very ambivalence means that sometimes we need to be urged on by a sense of fear. Again we see Julian's wisdom. Every now and again we need to reflect on our powers for self-destruction.

But we make our "humble complaint." The awareness of our fragility certainly makes us humble. We know that we can turn away from our true selves and self-destruct. So it is not too strong a word so say, as Julian does, that we offer our "complaint" to God. Often our prayer is "out of the depths..." as the psalmist says. And God's answer? Here Julian allows a host of images to jostle together—all that is meant by mothering comes to our aid, the whole life of church and sacrament; the "sprinkling with the precious blood" suggests both the vitality of our baptism and the daily food of our Eucharist. This makes us "pliable and tender"; the hardened heart is replaced by the heart of flesh; a new heart is created within us. Accepting the reality of our own sinfulness makes us more humble, humane, compassionate. We can no longer judge others; we know that we ourselves deserve judgment; we know our place is alongside the publican in the temple; we are purged of arrogance.

This work of humanizing is synonymous with making us more nearly the likeness of the God in whose image we have been created. But it is a restoring process that takes time, Julian wisely reminds us. Yet we know how difficult it is to accept the mystery of our own growth through time; we constantly seek instant solutions and immediate improvement. God has other methods, other ways. We have been given the gift of time. Sometimes we cling tenaciously to it and wish it would not slip away. At other times we try to swim against the current and go back in time but we cannot store it and we cannot retrieve it. Nor indeed can we hasten it; we can only use it to the best advantage. To use this moment as well as we might is all that we can do. No one has reminded us of this fact so well as the eighteenth-century French Jesuit, Jean-Pierre de Caussade. In his celebrated work, *Self-Abandonment to Divine Providence*, he describes the present moment as a "sacrament" that is "always full of infinite treasure" so that "everything is significant." For the believer there is no trivial time, no empty time, no useless time—if we are alive to the possibilities before us. De Caussade sums it up by saying: "There is no moment at which God does not present himself under the guise of some suffering, some consolation or some duty."

So our faith prompts us to make the best use of each moment of time, yet we know the total work of restoration, healing, and growth is God's work; it is in his hands.

God will never cease this "sweet and lovely work" until we are "born and delivered," as Julian says. So she brings us back to the image of God as mother. Time well used in a womb in which we are being fashioned, and this time is in God's keeping. The pain and thirsting of Christ are the cost of his mothering. So we learn the art of accepting the gift of time, we seek to use it as well as we might, and we pray to see it in the light of God's healing and saving purpose.

Time both tests and strengthens our love for God. St. Gregory the Great remarked:

> If desire for God is ardent, it is also patient. It grows under the trial of time. One must learn to wait for God in order to love him more, and to take advantage of the passage of time to become ever more open to his infinite plenitude.

CHAPTER 24

Waiting Patiently

(The Fifteenth Revelation)

It is God's will that we should take his promises and his consolations as generously and comprehensively as we can, and at the same time take the waiting and the discomfort as casually as possible, as mere nothings. The more casually we take them, and the less store we set by them for love of him, the less will be the pain we experience, and the greater our thanks and reward (Chapter 64).

As we become more accustomed to the things of God, the less concerned we should be about much that can engage our attention. All of us have numerous fears and ambitions, dislikes and interests. Sometimes these can distract us and at times lead us astray into the paths of foolishness and sin. But each time we return to the center way and reset our sights on the things that really matter, we are being gradually weaned from all that is trivial, unproductive, and self-destroying. The things that entice us are slowly becoming less self-centered and more and more purified. That is to say, they are being slowly turned from self toward God and others.

This process is bound to be a painful one at times, and so we need to be reminded that we are involved in a process of growth. In Chapter 64 Julian has another strange image of this growth. She "saw" a body lying on the ground, "without shape or form, a swollen mass of stinking flesh." This is a very ugly and unusual image for Julian, but one must remember the ugliness to which people had become accustomed at the time of the Black Death. Suddenly out of this body stepped a "most beautiful creature, a little child, perfectly shaped and formed."

This image prompts us to remember our growth as a transfiguration. There may be pain and suffering, and confusion and failures. At times nothing seems to be happening, but the leaven is at work. It all does have a purpose. In faith we affirm the presence and dynamism of a transfiguring power at work within us, though it remains largely hidden from view. The transfiguration of our Lord affords us some hints of what is happening. Not only did his face shine like the sun, but his clothes became whiter than any earthly bleach could make them. Divinity was touching humanity and the whole natural world, and making all things new in Christ.

In the same Chapter (64) Julian recognizes our continual weakness, "our old inertia and spiritual blindness." So often we seem far removed from the idealism of Christianity, so little touched by the mystery of transfiguration. Yet, Julian reminds us, "God's will is for us to know that he has not forgotten us."

So we accept the mystery of this time-process of transfiguration along with our own frailty and weakness. When we keep our minds fixed on the great reality of our life in the Trinity then we can accept the fluctuations and mystery of the process with a casualness and good humor. We can pray to be "of good cheer" and have a joy that is full.

In the collection of correspondence entitled *Letters to an American Lady*, C.S. Lewis has a moving image that aptly sums up this attitude of patiently waiting in a casual manner. On June 28, 1963, in one of his last letters, he wrote:

> Think of yourself just as a seed patiently waiting in the earth; waiting to come up a flower in the Gardener's good time, up into the *real* world, the real waking. I suppose that our present life, looked back on from there, will seem only a drowsy half-waking. We are here in the land of dreams. But cock-crow is coming. It is nearer now than when I began this letter.

In some strange way as we become more patient with time, we also become more detached from it. We are being slowly schooled in the truth that we don't have here a "lasting city," that our hearts are only going to be satisfied with something Other.

CHAPTER 25

Rough Passage

(The Sixteenth Revelation)

This word, "You will not be overcome" was said very distinctly and firmly to give us confidence and comfort for whatever troubles may come. He did not say, "You will never have a rough passage, you will never be over-strained, you will never feel uncomfortable." but he did say, "You will never be overcome." God wants us to pay attention to these words, so as to trust him always with strong confidence, through thick and thin. For he loves us, and delights in us; so he wills that we should love and delight in him in return, and trust him with all our strength. So all will be well (Chapter 68).

At the end of Chapter 65 Julian remarks that the whole fifteen revelations were given on that one special day from four in the morning to after three in the afternoon. The sixteenth revelation took place on "the following night" and it "concluded and confirmed all the previous fifteen" (Chapter 66).

It is very clear in Chapter 66 that Julian felt exhausted

and emotionally drained after that deep and prolonged prayer experience. She is quite clear that during her sleep she had a vision of the devil. This experience was a frightening and unnerving one and she remembered her former prayer experiences and "to that I fled for comfort (and) felt a great peace and rest." She is reminded that God is with her. There are moments when we see need to recall God's past favors and presence.

Her experience also shows us that soon after our moments of great prayer, and hot on the heels of our great achievements, we can speedily be reminded of our frailty. We can only boast in the Lord, not in our own strength or accomplishments. We are reminded of St. Paul's experience: "I will all the more gladly boast of my weaknesses, that the power of Christ may rest upon me. . . .When I am weak, then I am strong" (2 Corinthians 12:9-10).

As we place our weakness alongside Christ's strength, we are again challenged to be patient, to allow the process of growth-through-time to run its course. Sometimes we have to be content to remain patiently with the pain, and the failure, and the weakness. One is reminded of the incident in the storm-tossed bark as told by the synoptics. Our Lord was asleep; the storm seemed to threatening and the boat so fragile. When he stilled the storm in answer to their pleas, our Lord challenged their faith: "Why are you afraid, O men of little faith?" (Matthew 8:26). To have faith means to be prepared to stay with the storm, to endure the frailty of one's bark, to accept vulnerability, to refuse to give way finally in the face of our emotional reaction or the frightening circumstances. Faith means a lifeline to the substance of God's love and fidelity, which remain hidden and obscure, often without much hint or suggestion. And again we come back to St. Paul's certainty: "My grace is sufficient for you; my power is made perfect in weakness" (2 Corinthians 12:9). But this is apparently something we can only learn from reflecting on a storm we have endured, just as St. Paul learned it from being harassed. It cannot be learned simply as a cozy theory.

So we pray for the grace to discern the true meaning of our painful and frightening moments, and our times of trial and challenge. The storms do have a purpose and meaning. As we view them from a distance, we do become more confident of a power beyond ourselves that strengthened and guided us through them. As time goes on we become more and more conscious of that same power within us in the present when we face another period of darkness and pain. The Christian can walk in the valley of darkness and know there is no cause for fear. At such times we learn trust and patience and confidence "through thick and thin."

CHAPTER 26

Becoming Wise, Gentle, Faithful

*Whatever his manner of teaching, his will is that
we should be wise enough to perceive him, gentle
enough to receive him, and faithful enough to
keep ourselves in him. For there can be no goodness in this life above and apart from our Faith,
and no spiritual help in anything less: so it seems
to me. But in the Faith is where our Lord wills us
to stay. It is by his work and goodness that we have
to keep ourselves in it; and it is by his permission
that we are tested therein by our spiritual foes, and
are made strong. For if our faith met no opposition
it would deserve no reward, if I understand our
Lord's meaning aright (Chapter 70).*

Julian's great prayer experiences did not free her from suffering. Indeed, she seemed to know more pain, darkness,
and temptation in these later chapters. She has not been
lulled into some gentle Platonic detachment. At the beginning of Chapter 69 she recorded yet another experience of
the devil. He came "with heat and stench" and in the face
of this ugliness and evil she turned to the cross. This was

evidently a prolonged battle with evil. She tells us that the "Fiend kept me busy all through the night." The awareness of evil, the struggle with temptation, the ease with which we can sin can indeed remain with us for prolonged periods. This very struggle is so vital a part of growth and transfiguration.

All the while, we are being taught to be wise enough to perceive the Lord. There can be no doubt about the growing wisdom of Julian. It becomes especially clear in these later chapters. St. Luke describes Jesus not merely as growing and becoming stronger but also being "filled with wisdom." He has become our wisdom (1 Corinthians 1:30) but he only becomes this in time. Wisdom is not merely knowledge. It is an ability to recognize evil, to perceive good and live well. This requires being schooled in experience, in allowing God to work in our lives. We perceive or discern the coming of the Lord, and that has about it a strong hint of the eucharistic doctrine of Paul in 1 Corinthians 11.

It is also clear that this God-given gift comes to the simple, the gentle, the childlike. It comes not to the worldly-wise but to those who are humble, receptive and in some sense "little" (Matthew 11:25-26). The original text appears to have the idea of receiving the Lord "sweetly"; we taste and see that the Lord is "sweet" (1 Peter 2:3-4). But the idea is much the same. We only discern and receive the Lord if we have a certain docility, openness, and gentleness. These are not weak, effete things but real signs of the presence of the Spirit. The whole passage suggests that we are being made more humane, more receptive, as we continue to be open to the Lord.

And finally this is not merely some passing fad. We must remain "faithful." Each day we need to be open to the teaching Spirit who alone can school us in wisdom; docile to the creative Spirit who alone can form a new heart in us. We must persevere. Fidelity to the quest is necessary if the growth is to be complete. And Julian makes it clear that this is not a weak, overly pious Christianity: We are being "tested...and made strong." However gentle her prose and courteous her approach, Julian never permits us to slide into mere sentimental religion. No one better than she can present the Christian life as a thing of great beauty and loveliness, but its vigor and strength are in no way impaired.

Perhaps this chapter prompts us back to the Eucharist as the center of our lives, the summing up of all that we do. It is there that we seek to discern the Lord's presence and his saving work; it is there that we must be gentle, open, and receptive as we approach his word and sacrament. It is the constant repetition of the eucharistic action that at once symbolizes and empowers that faithfulness and perseverance we need so much. That is not merely a gift for each of us for ourselves; it is also a gift to minister to a world that is so much in need of it.

This living and motherly touch of God in the Eucharist makes us safe. The old prayer of the Roman liturgy for the reception of Holy Communion spoke of our being "kept safe" (custodiat) by this sacrament until we reach eternal life. As we grapple with the problem of evil, we have this remedy "to be aware of our wretchedness, and fly to our Lord." We know that our Lord "is almighty and may punish me mightily; he is all-wise and can punish me wisely. And he is all-good and loves me most tenderly (Chapter 77). And again we have a reminder of our true home being within the Trinity.

> Flee to our Lord and we shall be strengthened. Touch him, and we shall be cleansed. Cling to him, and we shall be safe and sound from every danger...we should be as much at home with him as heart may think or soul desire (Chapter 77).

CHAPTER 27

A Real God

Some of us believe that God is almighty and may do everything; and that he is all wise, and can do everything: but that he is all love, and will do everything—there we draw back.

As I see it, this ignorance is the greatest of all hindrances to God's lovers (Chapter 73).

A true belief in God involves us in real-life decisions. Julian has been given special prayer experiences by God, but as we have seen she was very clear that such experiences did not make her a holy, faithful person.

The fact that I had this revelation does not mean that I am good. I am good only in so far as I love God the better (Chapter 9).

The real test of our love for God involves us in practical choices, in making clear and definite commitments to a particular manner of acting. The knowledge or the "prayer experiences" we have are not necessarily signs of human goodness and growth. The basic choice that we all have to make is the choice between what is good and what is manifestly evil. The choice is not simply made once and for all;

it has to be repeated and renewed. Julian was faced with this same challenge. On a second occasion she was tempted by the devil. Again, her language is at once colorful and graphic, yet her description of personified evil has nothing exaggerated or frantic about it. Nonetheless, the frightening possibilities are clear; the experience was "calculated to drive me to despair." Again, Julian returned to the basic truths: "The cross which had been my comfort previously" and the "creed of Holy Church" and "my heart I fixed on God, with all my trust and strength." The storm of temptation lasted "all through the night" (Chapter 69).

Thus the real follower of the Lord will be the one who makes practical use of the faith, who perseveres despite the temptations and challenges. To persevere one must have the help of God. It is all too easy to reduce our belief in God to a mere theory, to give verbal recognition to God as one who *may* and *can* do everything. In such cases we have removed God to the detached bystander. This attitude has permeated much Western Christian thinking since the Enlightenment. Such an attitude is close to that of the Deists; such a view of God does not have God vitally involved in creatures. A real belief involves being able to accept that God is deeply concerned and present in *my* world, that God lovingly enfolds and embraces the world in which I live.

To have such a view involves one in hearing the word and doing it. The certitude of faith such as Julian had does not come merely from reading or study (though that might help); it does not come from what we can appreciate or articulate (though we might be called upon to do so): It really depends on the decisions we make, the choices we opt for, and the way we act.

Julian recognizes that we can draw back from a living commitment because of dread. And in Chapter 74 she analyzes what this dread might mean and shows how it can be progressively purified until it comes to mean a "dread born of reverence," which "pleases God. It is so gentle."

The image she reiterates is the idea of mother. So the (at times) frightful struggle with evil is from our point of view a gradual deepening of commitment and a struggle to make the right choice between good and evil. At the same time it is also a gradual revelation, a deepening of the experience we have of being born anew into the life of the Trinity. This fundamental doctrine is no longer merely a theological or doctrinal statement: It is something we live, with certainty. This is the result of God thirsting for us (Chapter 75).

And so Julian teaches us something about our own journey into God, and about the manner in which we need to have compassion for others and a godly longing for their growth as Christians. We know what is involved in the struggle to cooperate with God's self-revelation. We can be held back by all manner of weaknesses and fears. As we learn to make God more real, we also learn what it is to be human. For the Christian this must mean not so much being learned as being compassionate to others journeying on the same way.

For the Christian man or woman of prayer, this journey into God involves a growing self-knowledge and a deepening compassion for others. We come to know the deepest truths about the human condition and its need for "saving." Here in the heart of contemplation is the dynamism for action: the love of God being poured into our hearts. That is a love we must share. We are being prompted and challenged to be more concerned for others, to be more involved in the pain of the world.

CHAPTER 28

All Things Working Together for God

In this life man is able to stand because of three things; by these same things God is worshipped, and we are helped, kept, and saved. The first is the use of man's natural reason; the second, the everyday teaching of Holy Church; the third, the inner working of grace through the Holy Spirit. All three come from the one God. God is the source of our natural reason; God the basis of the teaching of Holy Church; and God is the Holy Spirit. Each is a distinct gift which we are meant to treasure and to heed. All of them are continually at work in us leading us Godwards. These are great things, and God's will is that we should know something about them here below: to know the ABC as it were, and have the full understanding in heaven. All this will help us on our way (Chapter 80).

There is more here than a hint of the Trinitarian nature of the whole of our experience. This delightfully structured paragraph also shows Julian's comprehensive and balanced approach to life. A human being is able to give a meaning, unity, and sense of purpose to life, which is not merely a constant, meaningless flux. That wise old man, Marcus Aurelius, recognized the challenge and the possibility of giving it all a value and a purpose when he wrote his *Meditations:*

> An empty pageant; a stage play; flocks of sheep, herds of cattle; a tussle of spearmen; a bone flung among a pack of curs; a crumb tossed into a pond of fish; ants, loaded and labouring; mice, scared and scampering; puppets, jerking on their strings—that is life. In the midst of it all you must take your stand, good-temperedly and without disdain, yet always aware that a man's worth is no greater than the worth of his ambitions.

We are called upon to give a meaning to life. For people in the Judeo-Christian tradition, there is a very strong tradition of seeing the "natural reason" of humankind as containing something from God.

> For this commandment which I command you this day is not too hard for you, neither is it far off. It is not in heaven, that you should say, 'Who will go up for us to heaven, and bring it to us, that we may hear it and do it?' Neither is it beyond the sea, that you should say, 'Who will go over the sea for us, and bring it to us, that we may hear it and do it?' But the word is very near you; it is in your mouth and in your heart, so that you can do it (Deuteronomy 30:11-14).

Calvin in his *Institutes* maintained that "some sense of the Divinity is inscribed in every heart" and Newman said conscience "implies a future and witnesses the unseen." In our pilgrimage Godward we can be confident that the practical decisions we make are good and grace-bearing. Often we can be dismayed and perplexed because we cannot decide between several options, or having decided on one, others suddenly seem more suitable and indeed more godly. Unless we are very sure that the decision has been a wrong one and likely to lead to evil, we must be at peace with our decisions and carry the cross involved in living them out. Provided we have sought the guidance of the Spirit and have looked squarely and reasonably at the issues involved, then God has been with us in the decision we have made and will abide with us in living them out, making them saving, grace-bearing things.

In all this we are "helped, kept and saved" by the second manner in which God is revealed to us: in the life and ministry of the church. The "everyday teaching of Holy Church" sums up all that Julian has been teaching about the church. Although it can sometimes be "shaken at the world's sorrow, anguish, and tribulation" (Chapter 28), it is a real revelation of God (Chapter 30) for it is *his* Holy Church. God is its foundation, its being, its teaching" (Chapter 34). And as we have seen, it is here we experience the mothering of God (Chapter 61).

Thirdly, Julian speaks of the "inner working of grace throughout the Holy Spirit." Very often Catholics have been fearful of this kind of language. To people of the Counter Reformation tradition, such talk would have seemed perilously close to the "private interpretation" favored by the Reformers. An optimistic and hope-filled view of the individual's religious experience seemed dangerous presumption. It is safer to look to the "teaching of the church for guidance."

Julian would have no doubts about accepting the teaching of the church. She has insisted on it in numerous places. But that does not exclude other means of revelation. God reveals self in our prayer life and we have been given the gift of the Spirit, whose temples we are. This positive aspect of Catholic teaching was kept alive by Austin Baker, who wrote in *Holy Wisdom:*

...the poorest, simplest soul living in the world, and following the common life of good Christians there, if she will faithfully correspond to the internal light...afforded her by God's Spirit, may as securely, yea, and sometimes more speedily, arrive to the top of the mountain of vision than the most learned doctors, the most profoundly wise men...the most abstracted confined hermits.

Julian is sure that each of these is a "distinct" gift; so one should not be surprised if there is tension and apparent conflict between the three. But that must be only apparent. The three are from the one God and are leading us "God-wards." We only know "something" about them here; full understanding comes later. As we struggle to avoid evil and do good, the three will surely come into clearer harmony and produce a growing wisdom and peace.

So we learn to be patient with ourselves and with the working of God's grace. In good time things do evidently come together. They are working toward harmony and peace, and our growing awareness of that is a measure of our growing in wisdom.

CHAPTER 29

Peace Beyond Understanding

Our faith is a light, coming to us naturally from him who is our everlasting Day, our Father, and our God. By this light Christ, our Mother, and the Holy Spirit, our good Lord, lead us through these passing years. The light is measured to our individual needs as we face our night. Because of the light we live: because of the night we suffer and grieve. Through this grief we earn reward and thanks from God! With the help of mercy and grace, we know and trust our light quite deliberately, and with it we go forward intelligently and firmly. When we are done with grief our eyes will be suddenly enlightened, and in the shining brightness of the light we shall see perfectly. For our light is none other than God our Maker, and the Holy Spirit, in our Saviour, Christ Jesus.

So did I see and understand that faith is our light in darkness and our light is God, the everlasting Day (Chapter 83).

At the beginning of Chapter 83 Julian expresses her confidence in the reality of her experience, which reflects the opening words of St. John's first letter. John had heard...seen and touched the Word. Julian, too, had "in some measure, both touch sight, and feeling of three of God's attributes...life, love and light." This is the foundation of all her experiences and runs through all the revelations. Her many years of reflection on these experiences enabled her to bring together every aspect of her pilgrimage so far. There is an interplay of light and darkness in ourselves and in our world. We are faced with conflict and division within and with the battle between good and evil in the cosmos. There is need for mercy and healing. Although the battle is not won, nor the pilgrimage completed, we know that we have sufficient light. This is our source of life. But we can't escape the suffering and the sorrow; there are dark sides to life. Realism forces us to face the fact. The same realism enables us to trust the light, life, love in which we are enfolded. We "know and trust our light quite deliberately, and with it we go forward intelligently and firmly." What strong vibrant faith! Julian is no vague, muddled, and overly pious old woman. She is deeply intelligent, and has a firm determination, which is the sign of a quiet, confident faith. This is no panic-filled reaction to the troubles of the contemporary world, or a fear of one's own frailty and sin. Julian has her sights set very squarely on the final meaning, the final transfiguration, when we will be "suddenly enlightened." Our light is "God, the everlasting day."

In the concluding chapters Julian manifests a great Christian maturity; her world has come together in a meaningful unity. The interplay of light and darkness does not unduly disturb her. The suffering and the joy can co-exist. A long-range view clothes everything in a purpose; we are journeying Godward, toward the complete transfiguration.

The faith that Julian exhibits is a mature faith. The God in whom she believes is not an arbitrary, hidden force, a remote and majestic God. The God of unspeakable loveliness whom Julian knows is also a homely God whose gentle love can best be understood by our feeble minds in terms of a mother's love.

Julian's maturity is also seen in her total commitment to this God who first loved her.

I saw for certain...that before ever he made us, God loved us; and that his love has never slackened, nor ever shall...(Chapter 86).

The total commitment to such love enables Julian to go forward "intelligently and firmly."

So we pray for this Christian maturity, this mature personhood, "to the measure of the stature of the fullness of Christ...no longer children, tossed to and fro..." (Ephesians 4:13). This is our heritage and our right as children of God.

Surely, it would be difficult to better this as a piece of religious prose. It is an apt vehicle to express the manner in which Julian remained faithful and experienced the peace beyond understanding; the conflicts and the challenges do not lessen. But there is a growing, confident certainty of the grace of God, and with Julian this presence of God is expressed in a homely and gentle language that could hardly be surpassed. So all aspects of life come into a harmony, and the harmony is the revelation of the God who enfolds and embraces us, and in so doing heals us and gives us an inner peace. And what was God's meaning in all this? Julian supplies the answer:

Know it well. Love was his meaning (Chapter 86).

Franciscan Spiritual Center
6902 SE Lake Road Suite 300
Milwaukie, OR 97267-2148